Exploration into Goodness

*Also by Frank Wright and
published by SCM Press*

The Pastoral Nature of the Ministry
Pastoral Care for Lay People
The Pastoral Nature of Healing

FRANK WRIGHT

Exploration into Goodness

SCM PRESS LTD

British Library Cataloguing in Publication Data

Wright, Frank, *1922* –
Exploration into goodness.
1. Christian ethics. Virtues
I. Title
241'.4

ISBN 0–334–00423–3

First published 1988 by
SCM Press Ltd
26–30 Tottenham Road, London N1 4BZ

Typeset by J&L Composition Ltd,
Filey, North Yorkshire
and printed in Great Britain by
Richard Clay Ltd, Bungay, Suffolk

Contents

	Prologue	1
1	The Attraction of Goodness	3
2	The Vision of God and Goodness	17
3	Spontaneous Goodness	27
4	Goodness as Loving	35
5	Goodness as Integration	43
6	Goodness as Invisibility	53
7	Nurturing Goodness: In the Church	61
8	Nurturing Goodness: The Experience of C.S. Lewis	67
9	Nurturing Goodness: In the Young	75
	Epilogue	83
	Notes	85

Prologue

No wonder my friends raised their eyebrows when I said that I was writing a book on goodness: it was almost as if they thought it typical of my arrogance. How could I possibly claim any expertise in that subject? Obviously, I couldn't. So although I write with almost passionate conviction, what I write is in the nature of an exploration and an invitation. Exploration, because for several years, there has been a deafening silence on the subject of goodness in those areas of theological and church life from which some such study might come. (It is ironic that my chief academic inspiration has been an agnostic philosopher and novelist.) Invitation, because my hope is that those more competent than I am will pursue the subject at greater depth and with greater rigour, with especial reference to its philosophical, psychological and New Testament background.

I have chosen goodness rather than holiness, not only because two excellent studies of holiness have recently been written,[1] but also because whatever the intimate connection between the two, goodness has the power to strike deep into the popular mind, and transcends any ecclesiastical boundaries. Holiness, on the other hand, has about it a forbidding, church-y flavour, a wrong sort of set-apartness, the very opposite of the attractive power of goodness. For this reason, I trust that my book will encourage and stimulate people from many different backgrounds within the church to focus on a subject which, whatever the current neglect, must surely have a central place in Christian faith and life. I especially hope that it will be useful for adult education groups.

Exploration into Goodness

My thanks are due to those students in university extra-mural classes around Manchester who, in our discussions on the subject, have helped to clarify my mind on certain issues; to BBC North West and Granada TV, for generously allowing me space on the air to explore different aspects of goodness; but most of all, to those many people who in their various individual ways have not only taught me but showed me glimpses of that goodness, which have so much encouraged me in my pilgrimage.

Just over three hundred years ago, Thomas Traherne, the metaphysical poet and divine, expressed perfectly the intention of this book, even if the writing falls short of that intention:

> I do not speak much of vice which is far the more easy theme, because I am entirely taken up with the abundance of worth and beauty in virtue and have so much to say of the positive and intrinsic goodness of its nature. But besides, since a straight line is the measure both of itself and of a crooked one, I conclude that the glory of virtue, well understood, will make all vice appear like dirt before a jewel, when they are compared together.

1

The Attraction of Goodness

Surely the attraction of *evil* would make more sense? Our present neglect of goodness is largely due to our contemporary fascination with evil in all its forms. Browsing round one of the country's leading bookshops the other day, I had difficulty in finding any examination of the phenomenon of goodness; but there, well displayed, was a recent book by the philosopher, Mary Midgley, with the simple title, *Wickedness*.[1] Evil is so prevalent and pervasive, so relentlessly portrayed in the media, that the possibility and attraction of goodness is clouded over. A subtle trick of evil is precisely that: to make us obsessive about it, so totally preoccupied with it that everything else gets crowded out of our lives. It persuades us to personalize it in the name of Satan and give it human qualities. And continuous exposure to evil has the inevitable effect of making us less sensitive, and so less able to perceive or appreciate the oblique and quiet examples of goodness which sometimes lie just around us. The most widely-used medium of communication today, television, is so much better at conveying the cruder and starker, more violent emotions of evil, hatred and jealousy than the gentler qualities of goodness, that there is little or no stimulus and encouragement to us to focus on goodness. And because it largely deals in fantasy, the medium has an in-built difficulty. As Simone Weil put it:

Nothing is so beautiful, nothing is so continually fresh and surprising, so full of sweet and perpetual ecstasy, as the good; no desert is so dreary, monotonous and boring as evil. But with fantasy it's the other way round. Fictional good is boring and flat, whilst fictional evil is varied, intriguing, attractive and full of charm.[2]

Such fascination with evil and difficulty in seeing the good isn't wilfulness: it goes back to our early childhood, where we quite naturally developed an interest in those things which were forbidden us, and considerable antipathy to anything which spoke of conformity, obedience or merely 'being good'. There is a further difficulty: it isn't only in fiction that goodness is often presented as boring and flat. Exhortations to being good (that is, being *moral*), not only in children but also in adults, often lack the excitement and the appeal of a journey of discovery in which the goal is always real, but never fully attainable. 'When ye shall have done all the things that are commanded you, say, we are unprofitable servants' (Luke 17.10). I recall that in the days when I was responsible for talking to children at family services and the like, it was difficult to get beyond a very well-worn path of modern heroes and heroines of goodness: Florence Nightingale, Albert Schweitzer and so on. (Most readers, I suspect, could finish the list for themselves.) It wasn't only due to my lack of imagination: it was essentially because goodness is of a shy and retiring nature and can easily be deformed by public exposure. (Isn't this why good religious television always has a problem? Some of the people whose lives are most illustrative of goodness are those who would rightly be most reticent about any self-advertisement – and in any case, there are perhaps only a few television producers who could handle the material with sufficient perception and sensitivity.)

A more radical reason why evil is so powerfully portrayed is because it often seems as if it is inbred, part and parcel of the fabric of creation. Consider how the animal kingdom has built into it the giving and receiving of pain; how the human race contains such an enormous potentiality for destructive power, individually and collectively; how death is the inevitable destiny of everything in creation. Evil seems to be far more insidious and enduring than any particular evil we could ever mention; but goodness? However firm its roots, it seems tender and spasmodic by comparison, even when we are convinced by faith in the resurrection that goodness has within it a power that doesn't merely ensure its ultimate triumph over evil, but also transforms evil situations into occasions of good.

Nevertheless, when we've spoken the last word about the power of evil, it is equally true that even when we've neglected it, sentimentalized it or just scorned it, goodness has a haunting quality which has been with us ever since we were told our first fairy-tales, and we saw ourselves alongside our heroes in their triumph over evil and wickedness. It's a quality which perhaps we've glimpsed from time to time in just one or two people and which has opened up to us, however fleetingly, another dimension, another world, far removed from the cynicism, carelessness and indifference which is often our daily experience. I think that most of us, when we meet real goodness – in some well-known saint, or some unknown man or woman – know that it matters supremely. We often pay lip-service to the power of goodness: saying, for instance, of the Sermon on the Mount, even when we've no time for religious dogma, 'Now if only we were all like that ... !' And outside the confines of strictly Christian faith, consider a man like Gandhi who, despite his commitment to unpopular causes like non-violence and his quirks of character, exerted a magnetic influence far beyond India, as Richard Attenborough's film testifies. There's a wistful attractiveness about goodness, even when we're inwardly doubtful about its effectiveness – and to all ages, too. I love the way in which the nineteenth-century writer, John Ruskin, at the age of four, preached to a congregation of empty chairs a sermon consisting of just three words: 'People, be good.'

St Thérèse of Lisieux is not at first sight a person who

displays the attractiveness of goodness, making a virtue of the suffering and invalidism she had to endure and looking forward to her death at the age of three. But in Monica Furlong's recent biography of her[3] she shows that the way in which Thérèse touched public imagination suggests a hope and longing in the unconscious of hundreds of people. She had, as a sort of eternal schoolgirl, a charm of innocence and goodness. So it was understandable that during the First World War, many French soldiers went into battle carrying her picture with them and that French airmen named an aircraft after her. It wasn't simply that they thought she would keep them safe and free from injury: it was that in the squalor and misery of the trenches, she held out some sort of promise that there is still a simple goodness on the earth which in the end, whatever the appearances, will prove more real than 'the hell on earth of the fields of Flanders'.

Curiously, this recognition of the universal attraction of goodness finds its expression in some very unlikely places. Some modern novelists and dramatists have caught Christians bathing and run away with our clothes – because they are *their* clothes as well! There is more and deeper examination of goodness in modern secular literature, I would claim, than in much contemporary theological writing – and that despite all the prevalence and pervasiveness of evil.

A good example of the way in which the haunting dream of goodness rarely disappears, even in the midst of the most sordid circumstances, is movingly illustrated in Dennis Potter's play, *Sufficient Carbohydrate*. Jack Barker is a man for whom everything is going wrong: his job, his prospects, his marriage. But every now and then, he is able to see his life in the light of a greater good, the symbol of which is a cargo boat which appears on the horizon early in the morning.

Trouble is, it reminds me of something else, too ... Something gone for ever or awaiting me for ever ... It's all like when the world began, and God Saw That It Was

Good ... For a moment – a whole minute – it's all so perfect you want to reach out and – pull it into your soul. You want to pick it all up – and *eat* it.[4]

This longing for goodness which Jack seems to have felt sometimes becomes translated into reality, even in politicians! In the fifties, Adlai Stevenson was the unsuccessful Democratic candidate for the Presidency of the USA. Here's Alistair Cooke's description of him:

> What he left behind was something more splendid, in a public man, than a record of power. It was simply an impression of goodness. He had mastered the art, far more difficult and rarer than that of a successful politician, writer, musician, actor: success as a human being.[5]

Alistair Cooke's phrase 'success as a human being' makes me conscious of how often we think of being successful at something or other and of how rarely we think of that most fundamental success of all: that of being a human being. The description of Adlai Stevenson is remarkably similar to another, but a very different sort of fictional character – and interestingly, despite my previous strictures on television's inability to portray goodness convincingly, this was one notable exception. I mean, of course, Anthony Trollope's final word in *Barchester Towers* on the character of Mr Harding:

> The Author now leaves him in the hands of his readers; not as a hero, not as the man to be admired and talked of, not as a man who should be toasted at public dinners and spoken of with conventional absurdity as a perfect divine, but as a good man without guile, believing humbly in the religion which he has striven to teach, and guided by the precepts which he has striven to learn.[6]

'A good man without guile', a description reminiscent of Luke's description of one of my favourite saints, Barnabas: 'a good man, and full of the Holy Ghost and of faith' (Acts 11.24). Not clever or tough or smart, all the qualities so generally admired today, and certainly not brilliant, but good. (I'm fond of Barnabas for another reason: he is also described as a Son of Encouragement, and one of the qualities of the good person must surely be that he or she encourages other people, and gives them *space*.)

To return to the literature of the twentieth century: I choose three examples of the fascination of writers with good in a world seemingly saturated with evil. Even when a writer on goodness disclaims as arrogance or pretence the possibility that he or she has penetrated very far into its heart, a danger still lurks in the shadows. Stevie Smith in her poem 'Away Melancholy' highlights this danger. At first she celebrates man's superlative nature:

> He of all creatures alone
> Raiseth a stone
> (Away melancholy)
> Into the stone, the god
> Pours what he knows of good
> Calling god, Good ...

and although he is 'beaten, corrupted, dying', man still

> ... aspires
> To good,
> To love
> Sighs ...

and so

> It is his virtue needs explaining
> Not his failing.[7]

But man's virtue, his goodness, cannot be explained, and the risk we run in exploring it is that of emptying something of its mystery by spilling words which in the end seem inadequate and superficial.

William Golding is a novelist best known for his realistic portrayal of original sin in the lives of different people, his conviction that, under their civilized veneer, there lies a potentiality for beastliness which is ready to break out at any time. Writing in the shadow of Belsen and Hiroshima, he claimed that man produces evil as a bee produces honey. So his novels seem grounded in pessimism, and we see what havoc is wrought amongst those choirboys on the island in *The Lord of the Flies*, by Dean Jocelin in his exaggerated ambition to build *The Spire*, and in the suffering of the burnt and handicapped Matty in *Darkness Visible*. But beyond his pessimism, Golding freely admits the possibility of creative genius, mankind's continuing ability to produce Beethovens, Shakespeares and St Augustines. And whatever the depth of pessimism and evil in his novels, there also appear characters with a quality of saintliness which goes some way towards redeeming the rest. So the real saviour in *The Lord of the Flies* isn't the naval officer who appears as the rescuing *deus ex machina*. It is Simon, the 'lonely visionary, the clear-sighted realist, logical, sensitive and mature beyond his years'.[8] So in *Free Fall*, Sammy Mountjoy searches for his lost innocence; Matty in *Darkness Visible* becomes the archetypal Suffering Servant; and even in *The Spire*, Dean Jocelin comes to some sort of mystical enlightenment as he sees the apple tree just before he dies. Out of the foulness and blackness of evil, and even in its very midst, the spirit of man (and hence of God?) is to be found in redeeming hints and glimpses of goodness.

A third example taken from modern literature is that of a writer whom we will explore further, as a philosopher as well as a novelist, later in this book, Iris Murdoch. In one of her latest novels, *The Good Apprentice*, she echoes the conversation in the novel *The Plague* by the atheist Albert Camus, between Tarrou, who organizes the sanitary squads to cope with the plague, and the doctor, Rieux. On a summer evening, they are both sitting on the terrace, sniffing the sea air and listening to the rattle of ambulances below, and Tarrou says that what interests him is how to become a saint. And when he is challenged by the doctor about this, since he doesn't believe in God, Tarrou replies, 'Exactly. Can one be a saint with God? – that's the problem, in fact the only problem I'm up against today …'[9] So in *The Good Apprentice* by Iris Murdoch, Stuart Cuno wants to become good – without God. He had this 'instinctive craving for nothingness which was also a desire to be able to love and enjoy and "touch" everything, to *help* everything'.[10] But God had always seemed, even in his childhood, an idol, 'something hard and limited and small … and certainly not the name of what he found within himself'.[11] So Stuart never went to church, although he sometimes sat quietly by himself in churches, for 'he wanted to heal people, he wanted to heal the world, and to get into a situation where this would be something simple and automatic, something expected every day'.[12]

That there can be goodness without God (or at least, without his presence being explicitly recognized) is evident in the most daunting and dire of human conditions, in life, I mean, and not only in literature. An incident in my own German prisoner-of-war experience shines out of the murk and drabness and greyness (and sometimes near-hopelessness) of that existence. It was the last winter of the war, and we were suffering the worst period of all so far as food shortages went. German transport had been badly disrupted by our bombing, Red Cross parcels were failing to get through, and there was a scarcity of rations all round. For some reason (perhaps connected with my considerable height) I seemed to lose rather more weight than others. Another aircrew member with whom I had an acquaintance, but didn't know well, must have noticed this, and one day, on returning to my bunk in hut 49B, I found a tin of meat-loaf awaiting me, with the words from the psalm written by the side, 'making thee young and lusty as an eagle, Alex'. ('Lusty' referred to the firm who made those meat-loaves!) Alex wasn't a Christian –

it was an act of goodness, in that sense, without God – but he had remembered from his Sunday school days in Argyllshire those words of the psalmist, and just thought them appropriate. He had saved that meat-loaf from the last consignment of parcels we had had, and I discovered later that it was the only tin he had left. Alex died tragically in his thirties, but his remembered act of generosity lives on.

The life of a concentration camp victim, of course, was much harsher than that of a prisoner-of-war, and you don't expect to find goodness in situations like that when men and women are desperate to survive, let alone live, and where just one unselfish act of generosity on your part over food may hasten your journey to the grave. Primo Levi was an Italian writer who had spent some time in Auschwitz concentration camp. In his book *Moments of Reprieve*, he collected stories of individuals who stood out against the tragic background of concentration camp existence, those who had the capacity and will to react to their bitter circumstances, and who accordingly displayed a 'rudiment of virtue'. One such character was Lorenzo by name, an Italian, and an eccentric in many ways, who at great risk to himself went into the camp kitchen on the sly at three o'clock in the morning to take anything that was left in the soup cauldrons in order to give it to two of his Italian friends. Without that extra, they wouldn't have been able to survive until the evacuation of the camp. The extra quart of soup helped to balance their daily calorie count. One morning, in the bitterly cold winter, Lorenzo arrived with the mess-tin badly bent and dented, and explained that the soup was a bit dirty. There were pebbles and grit in it, and much later, the recipients of that soup discovered that whilst he was collecting it, there had been an air-raid, and a bomb had fallen close to him and exploded. The mess-tin had been buried, and one of his ear-drums had burst. But Primo Levi then betrays the secret behind Lorenzo's perseverance: 'He had the soup to deliver,' he wrote. But the compulsion Lorenzo felt wasn't imposed on him; it was an inner compulsion of the spirit, the dynamic of goodness. And it was a goodness which amazed the two men as they ate their soup, for as one of them said, 'In the violent and degraded environment of Auschwitz, a man helping other men out of pure altruism was incomprehensible, alien, like a saviour who's come from heaven.'[13]

Now Lorenzo wasn't a saint, as that word is popularly misunderstood to mean: never doing anything wrong. Indeed, the whole concept of sainthood in the sense of a corps of the spiritually élite – let alone the process of canonization – needs a radical re-examination. For instance, one impression created by the word saint is that of a person who stands out as one of that corps of the spiritually élite, rather than of someone who, invisibly, is merged with one of the crowd. Often, the vocation of the saint is precisely the latter. The twentieth-century saint, Simone Weil, from whom we have already quoted, saw the essential religious task as being that of identification with suffering humanity, symbolized in her refusal, in the Second World War in this country, where she had taken up residence, to eat more than the rations afforded to each French Resistance worker. It was an identification, too, which prevented her from accepting Christian commitment on the grounds that it would mean belonging to an exclusive body which called itself 'We', as if it were over against, rather than an essential part of, humanity as a whole. Myra Schneider is a poet who works in a day-centre for physically handicapped adults. She illustrates in her poem *Belonging* how goodness will often show itself in the person who is an outsider:

> For I belong with those who don't belong:
> The eccentric, the oppressed, the over-sensitive,
> The voiceless struggling to communicate
> By finger; those beset by failure.
> Sufficient for me to find
> I slot into the human race.[14]

This identification with humanity, 'slotting into the human race', also highlights the difficulties we're involved in once we try to make people 'special' in the Body of Christ, those, for instance, to be canonized as saints. I remember reading some time ago about St Peter of Verona, often known as St Peter Martyr, who was featured in a well-known painting by Fra Angelico, and who was the Inquisitor for North Italy in the thirteenth century. He was assassinated by those whom he had charged with heresy. And when you think of the immoral methods of the Inquisition, its brainwashing techniques and its torture, you're bound to ask whether the heretics didn't serve the kingdom of God more than the Inquisitor. The church didn't canonize anyone who protested against the methods of the Inquisition, which did so much lasting harm to the cause of Christian faith in Western Europe. And we may wonder, too, why so many monks, virgins, widows and bishops are in the list of saints when laypeople, married women and ordinary priests hardly feature at all! In saying this, I am not indulging in a little anti-Popery. The Church of England experienced something of the same tension when it drew up the list of those to be included as lesser saints in the new prayer book: one newspaper reported the chairman of the Liturgical Commission as saying that failure to be included wasn't a sign of lesser saintliness: it was just that some were unfortunate enough to be born on the day when other saintly people were born as well!

So a clearly defined élite of holy ones, a hierarchy of merit however thinly disguised, won't do. Reticence about who is and who isn't a saint is as important here as it is elsewhere in the Christian life. And it is important not to confuse the popular misconception of saintliness as never doing anything wrong with goodness, for it is the very reverse of attractive. Like the word 'holiness', it can be off-putting and uninviting. For a long time, I had a cartoon on my office wall which depicted a middle-aged husband and wife engaged in a marital confrontation, and the husband leaning over the wife and saying, 'When anyone asks me what you're like, I tell them you're a saint – and that usually shuts them up!' But saints aren't only those who have reached some sort of moral perfection.

> If there is any meaning at all to the word 'saint', it may be that it describes people who are more, not less, human ... making false idols of saints or 'perfect' human beings is just a distraction from the task of loving the reality of humanity, and, I suspect, a distraction from having to face up to the reality of our own humanity.[15]

Even those best known, like St Paul, had conspicuous lapses, in that he was often touchy, vain and quarrelsome – not to mention possibly being extremely difficult to live with! The concept of moral perfection stemming from Christ's injunction, 'Ye therefore shall be perfect' (Matt. 5.48), has caused strong feelings of guilt and inadequacy in good people, who have not been helped to see that 'perfect' here denotes being 'rounded, complete and whole'. And the notion of 'perfectionism' in Christian history, which owes a lot to John Wesley's *Plain Account of Christian Perfection*, and which is a state of holiness in which attitude and motive are sinless, always recognizes the possibility of failings and weaknesses because of the frailties and limitations of fallible creatures. Perhaps we need to recognize that Christian maturity and moral perfection are not necessarily the same things, since any such maturity will have had to come to terms with the dark side of our nature, the almost cosmic battle that we all know within ourselves, even when we find it hard to admit it.

Like maturity, goodness speaks of a road, a journey, a pilgrimage, a direction of movement. If it spoke of something that had already been achieved, then complacency and spiritual pride would have set in, to deny the goodness which was the original goal. At least, saints and those whom we would see as good have this in common: a quality which isn't to do with the number of good deeds they perform, or their conspicuous lack of faults, but above all, with what they *see*. Looking back on my own life, the two or three people who have had most influence on me have had about them this mysterious power, and they'd all say they were very ordinary people. But it is ordinariness so transformed by what they've seen, that they become extraordinary. It is as if they're demonstrating something that comes from beyond themselves, as if they've seen something which grasps them and draws them like a magnet towards itself. Never self-satisfied, always travelling hopefully, even though they know they'll never finally arrive. But the journey, the pilgrimage is all and from time to time, intimations of their perfect goal shines through, and they become luminous with the luminosity of a power of goodness beyond themselves.

It is as if good people have seen something beyond themselves – but what? That must be our next exploration.

2

The Vision of God and Goodness

Picture yourself as a prisoner in a cave. You can only look forward because there's a chain round your neck preventing you from turning round. There's a wall in front of you, and a fire behind you. And in the light of the fire, you can see on the wall a shadow both of yourself and of any objects that are behind you. Prisoner as you are, you begin to imagine that those shadows are real, and you have no idea that there is anything in the world beyond the cave. But now just suppose that your chain were removed and you were able to turn round. You then see not only that the shadows aren't real, but also that there are steps leading outside the cave. And as you slowly and hesitantly start to climb those steps, you begin both to be drawn and blinded by the sun, which before you never knew existed.

Now, of course, this is an age-old allegory (slightly simplified) dating back from centuries before Christ, to the philosopher Plato. But it's an allegory that contains within it the secret at the heart of goodness. It spells out so clearly the only goal which makes sense of our lives and provides us with a sufficient dynamic in our pilgrimage.

Sitting down easily and comfortably by the fire, you may not want your cosiness disturbed: to know anything about yourself or other people or the world as a whole. You are content to exist, unaware. And to remain unaware is to protect ourselves from pain, from the trouble of response, from the business of being bothered, as well as from the joy of discovery and achievement. You have become a prisoner, then, of your own self-satisfaction.

But just suppose that the chain is taken away, and you're invited to enjoy a new-found freedom. You notice for the first time that the shadows aren't real; you begin to see yourself as you are; you come to some sort of self-awareness. You dimly recognize the psychological forces that play upon you, and make you the person that you are. But you are still in the cave, your horizons bounded by it. You may mistake the fire for the sun, and still think there is nothing beyond. So, to make the best of your life, you concentrate on yourself, even perhaps your 'self-improvement' by all sorts of techniques and therapies which offer you fulfilment; or if you are religious, by determined efforts of the will to overcome your selfish proclivities. Self-examination is always a dangerous process, unless it is seen in the context of something or someone larger than oneself, for it focusses the attention on the source of difficulty itself.

And all the time, beyond the cave, the sun shines and burns. Attracting us to make the steep ascent outside the cave is the source of all light and goodness, God himself. His light is so over-powering that it's difficult to gaze at him directly; but without him, we inevitably shrivel, and all the effort to make something of ourselves is doomed to failure. He is the attraction at the beginning of our steep ascent and the goal at the end; and as we're drawn by the magnetizing rays of his goodness, we see the sun-less situation in which we've been situated for the drab, dreary, unsatisfying thing it is.

The psalmist directs our attention and gaze towards God's dwelling place: 'O how amiable are thy dwellings: thou Lord of hosts; My soul hath a desire and longing to enter into the courts of the Lord: My heart and my flesh rejoice in the living God' (84.1,2), and again, 'Like as the heart desireth the water-brooks, so longeth my soul after Thee, O God' (42.1). However much it is obscured at present, this vision of God and his dwelling-place has always held a central place in Christian faith and tradition. 'The glory of God is a living man,' wrote one of the earliest Christian Fathers, 'and the life of man is the vision of God,' and so on down to the nineteenth-century hymn-writer F. W. Faber:

> Father of Jesus, love's reward
> What rapture will it be,
> Prostrate before Thy throne to lie
> And gaze and gaze on Thee!

'And gaze and gaze on Thee ...'

We are speaking, of course, of the spiritual activity of contemplation; and that might seem to indicate some esoteric activity reserved for the spiritually élite. But listen to what Iris Murdoch has to say in one of her philosophical works:

> I think there is a place both inside and outside religion for a sort of contemplation of the Good, not just by dedicated experts but by ordinary people: an attention which is not just the planning of particular good actions but an attempt to look right away from self towards a distant transcendent perfection, a source of uncontaminated energy, a source of *new* and quite undreamt of virtue.[1]

Perhaps one of the greatest barriers both to contemplation and to goodness is the notion that it is exclusively reserved for the few, and especially for the 'professionals'. But God told Moses to speak to the 'whole congregation of the children of Israel' about the necessity to be holy, and that incuded everyone, children as well. A spirituality which is not potentially available to all, or in other words, a *divisive* spirituality, is surely no spirituality at all. So whilst it's true that the advanced practice of contemplation may mark those most advanced in the spiritual life (the kneeling figure, for instance, entirely concentrated on the large cross in front of him), simple methods of contemplation are open to us all, wherever we are. At a time when many of us find difficulty in formal patterns of prayer and are becoming increasingly sceptical about the power of words, the wordless act of simply being still and looking at a natural object like a tree, a

19

flower or a picture, can help cultivate in us that contemplative spirit which (and this is the essence of the matter) takes us out of ourselves and fixes our gaze elsewhere than on ourselves. And if this seems too much for us in a life that we feel is always marked by muddle and chaos, even then we can still develop something of that contemplative spirit. For what matters is not the method we use, or perhaps the lack of method, but our recognition that wherever we are, we can be open to God, conscious of the way in which he is drawing us closer to himself, or drawing closer to us. Being open to him, stretching ourselves out to him as we would to the sunlight, knowing that wherever we are, he is there, if we are prepared to open our eyes and see. 'One of the principal truths of Christianity,' wrote Simone Weil, 'a truth which goes almost unrecognized today, is that the *looking* is what saves us.'

To pursue a vision is often sadly misinterpreted, as if the grandness of the concept ensures that the hard business of day-to-day living has been by-passed. Nothing could be further from the truth. It is precisely the 'looking' which keeps the attention fixed on the matter in hand, and stops it from sliding off into considerations of self-interest. And when the Christian life is seen as the life of 'attention', then the details of everyday life begin to matter profoundly. We too often give the impression that ethically, Christian faith is only interested in important contemporary social questions, whereas for most of us it is the humdrum that matters, finding what the truth is for us in the small and banal questions with which we live every day: how we are to make sense of our relationships, how much time we should give to our families, what our priorities in giving should be, and the like. But immersed as we all are in the routine of everyday living, the 'looking' which animates good people will help them to create a sense of space around them, the very reverse of the stifling piety which the notion of goodness often conjures up. Nor should the good person pursuing a vision be thought of as necessarily passive. Because there are values and more importantly, people about which he cares passionately, he will always be prepared to be a fighter, never dreamily sitting down in the face of injustice, or of anything else which indicates man's inhumanity to man. At the same time, his 'looking' will ensure that he sees the provisional nature of all that he champions, and even if that cause should finally be won, the vision will still lure him beyond the completion of that provisional task.

But if God is the source of all goodness, as Christian faith asserts, how can we say that he will be there in all circumstances – in the mess and muddle of human life, as well as in those moments when rapt in prayer he is drawing us like a magnet to himself? Thanks to modern psychology, and in particular the writings of Carl Gustav Jung, we have come to see the importance of recognizing the dark side of ourselves as well as the light. It is a false and ultimately damaging religion which simply asks us to recognize the light, the holy, the pious, and so makes us unconsciously project the evil, dark side elsewhere. True religion admits the necessity both to recognize that evil and dark side and to integrate it into personal freedom and goodness. It is easy for some forms of spirituality to protect us from evil and all the ambiguities of existence we experience every day and keep us in an artificial world. But God is not confined to that artificial world, his is the *real* world. (It is significant that in Plato's allegory, we only see the real world when we climb out of the cave and can look at everything in the light of the sun. Before, we were trapped in a cave of illusion.)

> For God is in everything and everything is in God, impersonal as well as personal; not merely the obviously beautiful and good, the intentional and meaningful, but the waste and void, the nebulae, earthquakes, sunsets, cancers, tapeworms.[2]

Ironically John Robinson, who wrote those words, died of cancer, and in his last sermon he reiterated even more strongly this truth:

For God is to be found in the cancer as in everything else. If he is not, then he is not the God of the Psalmist who said, 'If I go down to hell, thou art there also,' let alone of the Christian who knows God most deeply in the Cross.[3]

That is why we can make the strange, confident assertion that there is 'nothing in all creation that can separate us from the love of God in Christ Jesus our Lord' (Rom. 8.39).

That is the mystery we adore. When we are engrossed in some activity that we love, our absorption blots out all other thoughts and considerations. So in a real sense when we are taken up with the vision of God, when we contemplate the mystery (in the act, perhaps, of washing the dishes) we are put into a proper perspective. The better we're able to see God, the more this unregenerate and jumped-up self of ours is cut down to its proper size, no longer smudging everything it touches, no longer the ever-present ogre demanding rights, privileges, notice, attention. That I believe is the beginning of true goodness. It's no accident that true humility is the supreme hall-mark of the good person.

Humility is a rare virtue and an unfashionable one and one which is often hard to discern. Only rarely does one meet somebody in whom it positively shines, in whom one apprehends with amazement the absence of the anxious avaricious tentacles of the self ... The humble man, because he sees himself as nothing, can see other things as they are.[4]

But such humility can't develop if we're still stuck in the cave, contemplating simply our own navels, and being preoccupied with our souls. If we try to make ourselves more humble by saying to ourselves each day 'I must be more humble', we shall only succeed in making ourselves more self-centred still. That is one of the many paradoxes of humility. Perhaps you've heard of the author who continually asked his friends, 'Have you read my book on humility?', or the clergyman who, as he came down from the pulpit having preached a sermon on humility, said to himself, 'That wasn't a bad effort.' It is only as we make the steep ascent out of the cave that our eyes are continually drawn towards the sun, and we truly see ourselves for what we are in its light.

So humility isn't to denigrate ourselves, make ourselves out to be of no value in some sort of self-conscious way, almost telling everybody how humble we are. Rather, it is seeing ourselves in the light of the vision of God – and that means not taking ourselves solemnly or pompously, but ready to laugh at our own foibles and stupidities. Harry Williams put this well in describing the way in which to 'sit light to yourself is true humility'. 'For in laughter I accept myself not because I'm some sort of super-person, but precisely because I'm not. There is nothing funny about a super-person. There is everything funny about a man who thinks he is.' So 'thank God when you can take a delighted pleasure in the comic spectacle which is yourself, especially if it is yourself devoutly at prayer'.[5] Clifford Longley speaks of the way in which good people 'can sometimes be slightly daft; though many of them do manage to have their heads screwed on exceedingly tight. And unlike ordinary people trying to be pious, they can also be fun to be with.'[6] But the God whom we contemplate, who can help us to laugh at ourselves, is also the God to whom the hairs of our heads are all numbered, the God to whom each one of us has eternal value. So a *proper* self-love is part of a true humility; we are loving that which God loves.

Contemplating God and his goodness, then, isn't a one-way process: for just as we look to him for encouragement on the road to goodness, so he looks on us with love and tenderness.

He, then, who looketh on Thee with loving face will find Thy face looking on himself with love, and the more he shall study to look on Thee with greater love, by so much shall he find Thy face more loving.[7]

23

We may gaze and gaze in contemplation of God's majesty, but that majesty is the majesty of love, and as another verse in F. W. Faber's hymn says:

> Yet I may love Thee too, O Lord,
> Almighty as Thou art,
> For Thou hast stooped to ask of me
> The love of my poor heart.

The secret of goodness, I suggest, lies in contemplation, being drawn by the majestic rays of God's goodness, as we leave the cave, and make the arduous climb in the sunlight. Then we shall have a chance to *become* what we *see*. But the climb is arduous. We human beings are much more complex and enigmatic than we sometimes allow for religiously, and self-centredness much more subtle and diabolical. One reason why some people find a belief in goodness hard to sustain is because of their innate faith that it should produce some sort of tangible reward in this life, and we appear to be let down endlessly. 'Why did he have to die so young? He was such a good man.' And it is felt that the reward which is denied us for our goodness speaks of a lack of goodness in God. But the reward of goodness is being good. The notion that if we are good, God will protect us from all the ills and accidents of this life, as well as from death itself, dies hard. But die it must, for that is not the way in which his goodness works, in the promise of security and success. Rather, it lies in that of his sharing, his being with the creatures he loves in all their pains and agonies, even to the point of crucifixion.

So vision and contemplation require hard work on the part of those who see: they are as far removed from the popular concept of 'dreamy spirituality' or 'easy piety' as it is possible to be. We need to act on what we see, little by little, lest it turns sour on us and destructive. And all that, without turning our attention back to ourselves, or taking as it were our spiritual temperature all the time. For there is a paradox at the heart of all true spirituality. The more we go out of ourselves, the higher we climb out of the cave and into the sunlight, the more we grow in likeness to God, and the more human we become. On the other hand, the more we imprison ourselves in the cave, the more we enclose ourselves in self-interest, the less human we become. In other words, we become our true selves by always being ready to let go of ourselves.

A close friend of mine died recently. He had a remarkable propensity not only for mimicry (especially of Groucho Marx) but for laughing at himself as well. Chatting about him after his funeral, another friend said that 'even when he was making you laugh, it was as if his gaze were fixed somewhere beyond himself'. We didn't pursue that conversation, or try to unravel the mystery. But that remark illustrated again for me the essential quality of *seeing* in those in whom the power of goodness shines. Indeed, I find it helpful to translate the word 'sin' by 'blindness', blindness, that is, to God and to other people. Jesus 'opened the eyes of the blind' not only in a physical sense. And if we think of sin as blindness, we can then see the way in which there are deeper meanings in many of his miracles. It is our spiritual sight, and hence, insight, which constantly needs to be restored through our intimate contact with him.

In speaking of the late Archbishop Michael Ramsey, Clifford Longley said that he

> had the characteristic quality of a man of God, of seeming to be on such intimate terms with the Almighty. Such people give an impression that so sharp are their eyes of faith, they can actually *see* what the rest of us cannot: they can see God paying attention to their prayers.[8]

The more we give ourselves in contemplation of God, the less we shall need to try to make anything of ourselves; the more we lose ourselves – in him – the more we shall find ourselves – in him.

3

Spontaneous Goodness

It seems a long time ago since I had responsibility for a youth club; I am going back now to the late fifties. It was the era of the Teddy Boy and, although run by the church, the club was open and not confined to church members. We had a firm policy of not excluding anybody. So when a group of Teddy Boys appeared they weren't turned away. Looking back now, I see that their exhibitionism was designed either to impress or to terrorize the other members of the club. On this particular occasion, the group was bent on plaguing and terrorizing. It soon became clear that we were in for an ugly evening and some of the girls were getting scared. Before my simple mind had been able to weigh up the situation and decide what to do, the formidable lady who ran the canteen, affectionately known as Dotty, stepped in to the breach. She just walked quietly into the middle of the gang and without raising her voice one iota said to Terry, the leader, 'We don't have trouble here, we're here to enjoy ourselves', and then walked away. From then on, all became peaceful. Dotty's spontaneity had exactly the desired effect. She'd won a notable victory.

But it isn't, I'm afraid, a story of how we all lived together happily ever after. Two weeks later the group returned, and the air was more menacing still. Dotty tried to repeat her spontaneous action. Only it wasn't spontaneous any more. You see, she'd *calculated* that she'd be successful if she simply did again what she did the previous fortnight. Only this time, sadly, it didn't work: she was told in no uncertain terms where to go. The trouble was that Dotty had started

27

to imitate herself; she was no longer responding creatively to a new situation. In a word, she'd lost her spontaneity.

Remembering Dotty also reminds me of how easy it is for all of us, as the years go by, to slip into the way of *calculating* what we should do and how we should do it. We give a child a bag of sweets and, ignoring all those around, the child begins to devour them one by one – or even two by two! So we try to make the child share those sweets with others. 'Ask so-and-so to have one,' we say. And the child, grudgingly or not, responds. The victory is finally won we feel, when the same child on being given the sweets, *spontaneously* offers them to others. Such an experience of spontaneity at an early age has always lived with me. I was eight years old: it was the day of the Council School day trip to New Brighton, and we were gathered excitedly in the playground. My friend Jimmy then asked me how much pocket-money I had. 'Sixpence,' I said. 'I've got two-and-sixpence,' he said. And, instead of gloating over his superiority, he immediately did his arithmetic, adding the two sums together, dividing by two, and so equalizing our pocket-money at one-and-sixpence. And all as if it were the most natural thing in the world for anyone to do.

But such spontaneity, which we're so keen to develop in children and which we sometimes see in children like Jimmy, we somehow seem to lose as adult life creeps on. We're then tempted to work on a profit-and-loss basis, a nicely calculated more-or-less, and we comfort ourselves with maxims like, 'It's dangerous to let your heart rule your head' and 'You can be too generous, you know' and so on. *Goodness* doesn't lie that way.

Our growth in goodness depends on keeping or recovering the same spontaneity we've known as children when greater and perhaps tragic experiences of life and of other people develop in us that hard shell of self-preservation and self-concern. I was most moved by Mr Gordon Wilson's comment on receiving his New Year's Honours in 1988 after the death of his daughter in the bomb outrage at Enniskillin the previous Remembrance Day: 'I can't see there's anything unusual,' he said, 'it was quite a normal reaction for a Christian to make.' What he had done was to disclaim any feelings of bitterness and revenge towards his daughter's murderers; he had acted creatively and spontaneously.

Reflect for a moment: what is it in life which moves you in the depths of your being more than anything else? Isn't it when someone does something to or for you which you've done nothing to earn or deserve? Something which arises naturally and *spontaneously*, from the abundant overflow of a good and loving heart? It's the naturalness, the spontaneity which counts. And how repelled we'd feel if the other person were doing something superficially kind simply in order to impress us, or get themselves some Brownie points.

If we look for an example of spontaneous goodness in Christian history, we need look no further than St Francis of Assisi. He seems to have made himself immediately available to anyone or anything in creation: to the Saracen emperor, Saladin, to whom he preached, to the leper whom he spontaneously embraced, to the savage wolf he is reputed to have tamed. His life does not seem to have been directed by any explicit reference to the New Testament as such, and certainly not by any code. He seems to have simply responded in love to the moment. It is said that when bread was being handed round, he would always take the hardest and blackest piece; if there weren't enough beds for everyone, he would sleep on the ground; if there weren't enough blankets, he'd be the one who would manage without one.

Now the quality of this spontaneity as St Francis displayed it raises many questions, and above all, the question of 'loving God with the mind'. He does not seem to have admitted an appeal to the mind, or laid any store by mental reflection, even where the direction in which love as 'the inbuilt moral compass' was pointing was unclear. It is said that when his disciples totalled three in number, one of whom

29

was a rich man, he was uncertain as to what his new order should be about; so he knelt before the altar with a copy of the Gospels in his hand, and accepted as 'coming from the Lord' the passage on which his eyes first fell. He was quite clear that whilst meditation was essential for the nurture of the spirit, it was in no way connected with critical analysis or reflection and he seems simply to have believed that since meditation opens us up to God himself, all mental activity, as such, is superfluous.

Nevertheless, any qualifications that can be made about St Francis cannot obliterate the overwhelming influence he has had on Christian history ever since. And that, I dare to say, lies wholly in the attractiveness of his goodness, grounded in the spontaneity of a warm and loving heart to the Christ whom he perceived in all God's creatures.

So, if we're going to love with the whole of ourselves, our *heads* have a part to play. We're asked to love God with our minds. We can obviously make things worse for everybody in certain situations if we simply act spontaneously and over-generously without thought. For love is concerned with the best interests of the other person, and those interests might not be well served by such lavishness. But that, I suspect, isn't too common a fault. Much more usual is the way in which the springs of spontaneity have become blocked in us by world-weariness, cynicism and the hard crust of egotism which we develop in order to protect ourselves.

Natural as it may be to think of spontaneous goodness in this way, it is also true that Christian faith often exalts conformity above spontaneity. The churches 'esteem as a man of goodness not somebody (like Jesus) who challenges the ethical values and standards accepted as normative, but the man whose moral vision is confined within their limits, and who thus extols and advertises them ...' 'Thus is goodness confused with conformity and evil with the failure to conform.'[1] But once we take the road of spontaneity rather than conformity, we find that it is in some sense, a hard and insecure road. Because we are not conforming to some pre-established code, but are all the time being creative in our response to situations and to life, we are involved all the time in risk and uncertainty. Relying solely on the Spirit, we have no assurance that we are acting with absolute rightness. 'If we insist at all times on moral certainty, goodness becomes evil. Instead of being living and creative, goodness becomes static and destructive. That is why goodness often has such a bad name. We have all met people who are good in the worst sense of the word. Hence the people who rebel against the good can often be the people who bring about the realization of new forms of goodness.'[2]

So there can be no goodness without spontaneity. Often it seems to me that we present Christian faith as struggle, always choosing the hard path rather than the easy one, toiling away at good deeds and so on. And the Sermon on the Mount becomes a sort of impossible ideal we have rather despairingly to labour towards – the end of which must inevitably be a feeling of guilt or failure – or both!

I well remember how someone described the characters of two earnest missionaries at work in East Africa: 'They tried so hard, they became unlovely in their trying ...' Is it an accident that the same Greek word for 'good', used when Jesus describes himself as the Good Shepherd, is also the word for 'beautiful'? That is, the word for 'good' represents not so much moral rectitude but the attractiveness of goodness. As Archbishop William Temple used to say, it is possible to be morally upright repulsively! Our vocation is so to demonstrate the attractivness of goodness that men and women are won to it. The psalmist speaks of 'the beauty of holiness' and St John presents Jesus as 'good' in such a way as to 'draw all men unto himself.'

Surely the key to spontaneous goodness lies in the fifteenth chapter of St John's Gospel. Jesus said:

I am the true vine, and my Father is the husbandman.

Every branch in me that beareth not fruit, he taketh it away: and every branch that beareth fruit, he cleanseth it, that it may bear more fruit.

Already ye are clean because of the word which I have spoken unto you.

Abide in me, and I in you. As the branch cannot bear fruit of itself, except it abide in the vine: so neither can ye, except ye abide in me.

I am the vine, ye are the branches: He that abideth in me, and I in him, the same beareth much fruit: for apart from me ye can do nothing.

Notice that the fruit appears and ripens, quite spontaneously, when the branch abides in the vine. Can you see what this implies? That if we are truly in Christ, his life flowing through us as the sap flows through branch and vine, we shall produce the fruit of Christ-likeness without fussing or fretting, without being morbidly preoccupied with whether we're doing the right thing and so on. I'm no New Testament scholar, but the Sermon on the Mount has always seemed to me to be a wonderful and slightly whimsical illustration, sometimes exaggerated to make a colourful point, of what actually happens when a man is truly in Christ, when he reflects to others the love which he has first experienced in God-in-Christ. I think of it like this. We have a lovely Lancashire expression – keeping company with – and to me, Christian life is keeping company with Jesus. And when you keep company, you don't only share each other's life and concerns, you actually over a period of time and quite unconsciously, become like the one with whom you're keeping company. And you see, when that happens, we'll be ready, spontaneously, to go the extra mile, or to give more than the expected amount. We'll always be reaching out, seeking to express that love which we have, however dimly, seen in Christ.

There are, of course, dangers here as anywhere, and in the end perhaps it is a matter of emphasis. We might begin to claim too much for ourselves, we might let complacency set in, we might underestimate the weight of commitment involved in being spontaneous. But even a superficial glance at the way in which Jesus responded to different individuals from many and varied backgrounds – Zacchaeus, Mary Magdalene, the woman by the well, to name but three – is sufficient to help us see that any preconceived plan we adopt which doesn't make us feel on our pulse where the other person is, cannot be right.

Now that spontaneity of spirit which comes from keeping company doesn't happen suddenly. Donald Nicholl tells the story of how early one Sunday morning, he was out running in his track-suit on a road not far from Bethlehem. As he descended the steep path said to be the track along which Mary and Joseph travelled, he met four Muslim workmen making their way to the quarry above. They were walking in single file, and so close that he almost ran into them. He just shouted a greeting, but by the time he reached the last of the workmen, which was only four or five seconds after he'd appeared on the horizon, the latter had taken a large handful of raisins out of his lunch-bag, and pressed them into Donald Nicholl's hand saying 'You are sweating.' He couldn't stop as he was running so fast and could only just shout, 'Thank you.'

> There was a genuinely spontaneous action. It made me wonder how an obviously poor, uneducated workman could manage to do what in my experience I have found to be beyond the capacity of the finished product of our seminaries and universities ... It was only afterwards that I was given a clue by a Muslim friend to whom I recounted the incident. 'Pure heart,' he said. 'The man must have been faithful over many years in the practice of his faith to have such a pure heart.'[3]

Notice that last phrase: 'faithful over many years in the practice of his faith'. There is, in other words, no short cut to goodness. For the Christian, its nature depends on such closeness and intimacy with the person of Christ, keeping company with him through the hard disciplines of prayer, meditation, sacrament, and imaginative Bible-reading. Whatever means we choose doesn't so much matter: what *does* matter is the relationship, and our sustaining of that relationship. And the product of that relationship is not only naturalness and spontaneity – it's freedom and release as well.

4

Goodness as Loving

To recognize the mystery inherent in each human being is to penetrate the secret of goodness as loving. For to recognize the mystery is to begin to reverence – and to recapture the reverence for persons is perhaps the most sorely pressing need of the age in which we live. Whilst individuals' rights and interests are being fought for in all sorts of ways, at a time when small is considered to be anything but beautiful, those rights and interests are often only seen in practical terms: the reverence has departed.

We recognize the mystery, we reverence the person when we see them in all their uniqueness; and that can only happen, first, when we are not seeing them in relation to ourselves, and then, when we glimpse something of their eternal worth. That takes us back both to contemplation and also to the way in which we are to be 'in Christ'. Contemplating God involves us in contemplating and appreciating his creation, and everything in his creation. 'All things were made by him, and without him was not anything made that was made' (John 1.3). The more we're accustomed to the habit of contemplation, the more naturally we shall see other people for the distinctive, lovable people they are; the more we allow ourselves to be 'in Christ', the more we shall see them as he sees them, and recognize the 'incognito Christ' in them. 'Inasmuch as ye did it unto one of these my brethren, even the least, ye did it unto me' (Matt. 25.40). And the 'doing' spontaneously flows from the 'seeing'.

The uniqueness of human beings finds beautiful expression in the writings of Viktor Frankl, a psychotherapist who underwent in concentration camp some of the bitterest experiences anybody could possibly suffer. This made him ponder deeply on the meaning of love, and in his book, *The Doctor and the Soul*, he asks us to imagine a man who has lost the girl he loves for ever, either through death or permanent separation. He is then offered a double of his beloved, one like her in every way. So can he transfer his affection to this double – just like that? No, says Frankl,

> for the true lover does not 'care about' particular psychic or physical characteristics 'of' the beloved person, he does not care about some trait that she 'has', but about what she 'is' in her uniqueness. As a unique person she can never be replaced by any double, no matter how perfect a duplicate. But someone who is merely infatuated could probably find a double satisfactory for his purposes. His affections could be transferred without difficulty to the double. For his feelings are concerned only with the temperament the partner 'has', not with the spiritual person that the partner 'is'. The spiritual core as the object of the true attitude of love is, then, irreplaceable and inexchangeable for the true love, because it is unique and singular.[1]

'Unique and singular . . .' Goodness, then, is loving people not because of their attractiveness, their gifts, possessions, abilities or achievements, or even the lack of all these things. Goodness is loving people, because they *are*, in all their uniqueness.

Certain consequences immediately follow from such 'seeing'. Initially, it relates to the first and most intimate love-relationship in which we are involved, a relationship which will probably determine our capacity to love later on in life. If we get the mother–child relationship wrong, the consequences can be tragic for many years to come. But that relationship, we know, can go wrong, not only through a lack of love, but through a wrong sort of loving. I have sometimes thought that there should be a health-warning in every home: 'Families can damage you – emotionally.' In our churches we make great play of the family these days, with our family communion, family services and the like. (Incidentally, how welcome does *that* make the single, the divorced and the widow or widower feel?) But I sometimes wonder what connection all that has with Jesus himself. It doesn't appear as if he ever allowed the claims of his family to take precedence over the claims of his mission in life. The incident when he got lost in the temple at the age of twelve and caused his mother much embarrassment and anxiety seems to have set the pattern for the rest of his life. 'Who is my mother? Who are my brothers? Whoever does the will of God is my brother, my sister, my mother' (Matt. 12.48–50). Here we begin to glimpse, I believe, what families are for, what goodness in loving parents involves. We are placed in families to be given the emotional security which only unconditional love can give us. And only within such an unconditional, non-suffocating loving atmosphere do we have much chance of growing to our full stature as human beings, which is our purpose here on earth. Unconditional, non-suffocating love: those of us who are parents need to work ourselves out of a job. We should encourage the freedom and responsibility of our children, allow their mistakes, and only in the final analysis provide a safety-net of love and care. Any attempt directly to influence our children (or indeed, anyone whom we love) is always an attempt, however subtle, to make them extensions of ourselves. We never come to appreciate their individuality or singularity, we never know them as the unique, real persons they are.

Possessive love of any sort, in families, marriage and loving relationships always acts like a corrosive acid: it stunts human growth, sours and embitters, and in the end, denies true love on the part of the lover and the loved. As parents, we may want to mould our children to some preconceived model. As husband or wife, we may want our partner to fill some sort of idealized picture we have of him or her. Our

37

sometimes veiled instinct for power makes us want the other in some sense to be dependent on us: nothing feeds our egotism more. And when we see children beginning not to fit the mould any more or the marriage partner deviating from the idealized picture, then our temptation is to manipulate them, and make them return – and there are a thousand-and-one forms of manipulation!

Possessiveness may also involve us in exclusiveness. We do not allow our partners to be involved in other relationships, lest we lose them. The truth, however, is that the relationship would almost certainly be a richer relationship, were it not so exclusive, and if it were given the chance to be fed from other sources! The truly loving family is surely the family into which anyone from outside is not made to feel a stranger but warmly welcomed. In connection with relationships, I have spoken elsewhere of an essential truth about the much-maligned doctrine of the Trinity: that the circle of relationship it signifies isn't a closed circle, but one which is always open, and from which there is a stream of on-going love which draws us into the circle.[2] There is usually something wrong with a relationship where two or more people are entirely absorbed in it. 'If you love those who love you, what reward have you? And if you salute only your brethren, what more are you doing than others?' (Matt. 5.46f.). If of set purpose, we set bounds to our love in this way, we are negating its very nature.

A consequence, then, of our really seeing other persons in all their uniqueness, as Christ might see them, and as we recognize the Christ in them, is that we shall be prepared to let them be. And 'letting be' is possibly the most apt definition of love itself, and more apt than the impulse towards union with the beloved, which might be too egocentric. But 'letting be' isn't, of course, standing aside, detached, unconcerned. It means enabling the other persons to be the best of which they are capable and realize their full potential as human beings. And that could be very costly, since it might also involve the one who loves not only in letting be, but in letting go as well, or in other words, being ready to loose the ties that bind lover and loved together. It might be that in order properly to love a person, we may have to give up all human contact with that person, so that he or she can realize what there is in them to be.

The phrase 'Christian love' is often used, in contrast to 'natural love', as if it were essentially of a superior nature, and as if all lesser loves than 'Christian love' were to be devalued and possibly discarded. I find this difficult not only theologically, since God, the Holy Spirit is surely the source of all true love, but also unrealistic. It is surely significant that in the Bible the analogy of love between the sexes is used to expound the love of God. The prophet Hosea compares the love of God for Israel to love for an erring marriage-partner; St Paul compares the relationship between man and wife to the relationship between Christ and the church, and the Revelation of St John ends with a vision of the church as the bride of Christ. All these analogies would not, of course, have been possible if there were too sharp a distinction between 'Christian' love and other forms of love. Clearly, Jesus himself didn't make such a nice distinction, since he enjoyed such friendship with the 'beloved disciple' of St John's Gospel.

Recently, I took down a book I've had on my shelves for a long time: C. S. Lewis's *The Four Loves*.[3] And it reminded me of the distinctions we used to make, as theological students, between the different kinds of love. But when I look back now on those unreal distinctions, I realize how easy it was to deceive myself, as if I could dissect my character – isolate my will, for instance, from my feelings – and *make* myself love, even when I didn't feel like it! As if I were saying, 'I don't really care for you, but I'm jolly well going to love you, whether you like it or not, or whether I like you or you like me!' But if we *see* other people properly, loved by God and struggling against difficult circumstances, perhaps even

39

against their own temperaments, we at least have a chance of coming to like them more in time. Of course, we can't like everybody all the time, and there's no reason to feel guilty if we can't – but to make too sharp a division between loving and liking, for instance, is not only to restrict and confine human loving – it is to reduce it to a narrowness its nature denies. And if we are to make such distinctions, 'Christian love' above all has within it a dimension which widely transcends anything envisaged by human love. For it sees such love as extending to any one who is a neighbour, and a neighbour, of course, in Jesus's teaching is the one whom circumstances have brought near at any given time. He (or she) may and very likely will be a stranger, he may be quite an unattractive person, he may be of a different race or country or religion, he may even be an enemy. But his humanity is enough in itself to confer the status of neighbour. Life has thrown two persons together, and their very encounter contains the demand for love. Again, it will be a matter of seeing the person in all his or her uniqueness, with the eyes of Christ himself.

This exploration of goodness as loving takes on extra significance at a time when the dark prophecies about Aids need taking seriously and when the threat leads us to examine more closely the nature of loving relationships. 'Good' people are being increasingly urged to promote and answer a call for a return to 'absolute standards', and to reject any moral decisions which take the precise situation ('the facts of the case') into consideration, as being weak and wishy-washy. There is a tone of insensitivity and lack of compassion which mark this insistence on absolute standards which can only increase divisiveness. Of course, one reason why talk of Christian standards, ideals and beliefs is inadmissible is because the only absolute for the Christian, the absolute of love, will never be satisfied with being confined to such restrictive boundaries. Love in its generosity will always seek to go beyond them, lest their achievement leads to the deadliest sin of all, self-satisfaction. The mistake absolutists make is that of assuming that the demands of love are somehow easier to fulfil than the requirements of standards. There is no more demanding morality than that which is based on love – and it is only our sentimentality, our immature need to be 'definite', and hence, our debasing of the word 'love' which would persuade us otherwise.

So goodness as loving cannot simply insist on conformity to a certain moralistic standard, or see motivation and dynamic in personal relationships negatively; our stance will proceed from different assumptions. We will see, for instance, that the level of personal intimacy and sexual expression should coincide with the emotional level of the relationship between the two people and the commitment enjoined in it. There is always the danger of confusing those levels, and it is precisely this which has caused so many personal tragedies, implicit in one-night-stands and the contemporary prevalence of touching and embracing (good in themselves) which has sometimes led people further than they intended or further than the emotional level required. To confuse levels of physical expression is to encourage wrong expectations and to damage the people involved in those relationships. To see that sexual morality has to do with the implicit integrity of the right physical expression of the right emotional level is not to be stuck with a negative, prohibitive morality, but one which springs directly out of a proper reverence for the other person, made in God's image, and from the nature of love itself.

Carl Gustav Jung used to say that when people brought sexual questions to him they invariably turned out to be religious questions, and vice-versa. That is a connection we need constantly to affirm. What Christians believe about the love of God, and respect for persons made in God's image, and the qualities, gentleness and compassion – all these are reflected in our intimate relationships. The obvious truth is that the more we love God, the better we show ourselves in human love.

5

Goodness as Integration

Perhaps most people would see the good person, or at least, the 'relatively good' person (we must not let the unattractive saint appear on the horizon!) as the one who has taken on board, and acts on, a few basic moral principles: fair-mindedness, generosity, a readiness to forgive and so on. These, we think, are the principles which *ought* to direct us, and so we *ought* to make a great effort to put them into practice. But there's an inbuilt difficulty: in trying hard to put them into practice, we split ourselves into two. There is that part of us which is trying hard (the spiritual part) and there is that part of us (the emotional and physical) which is rebellious, and doesn't wish to be directed, or diverted. It was char-acteristically a British heretic in the fifth century, Pelagius, who thought that we could become good by a resolution of the will, by struggling harder!

We know, inwardly, that it doesn't happen like that, as the mountain of broken New Year and Lenten resolutions illus-trates. Of course, if we're strong enough characters we can discipline ourselves in certain practical ways – making sure we lose weight, going to bed earlier, and so on – but that discipline of itself doesn't ensure that we are people who are whole or integrated. Our emotions and our minds aren't necessarily in tune with each other. And despite labelling Pelagius a heretic, Christian faith, it seems to me, has down the ages gone on making the same mistake. I remember the agonies of torment and grief I went through as a young, and to be truthful, slightly pious adolescent, trying to keep under control what my body was continually asking of me – and I wasn't really helped by a manual for communicants, given to me at my confirmation, which had a form of Saturday night self-examination which put ten questions to me, one of which was: 'Have you had naughty thoughts since last you made your communion?' Another asked whether I'd been in a Nonconformist chapel this week – these were un-ecumenical days – and that question was rather easier to answer in the negative. Nor was the book I was later recommended to read of much help either: *The Mastery of Sex*, it was called.

What I painfully experienced as an adolescent, adult Christians have tried for generations to enforce. They have tried to impose on their bodies and emotions a set of rules (largely connected with 'Thou shalt not') which they imagined Jesus would ask of them. But their bodies and feelings have thought differently, and the result has been a sort of schizo-phrenia, in which the 'spiritual' was supposed to control the rest of us, but somehow, was conspicuously unsuccessful. And Jesus himself saw the danger of this division within us, when he reminded the disciples that a house divided against itself falls: it isn't simply that parts of us are warring against each other, preventing the possibility of any wholeness or integration, but also that our concentration once more is turned in on ourselves. That way lies spiritual death, not life, and certainly lack of any integration.

The resolution of the difficulty is blindingly obvious. It can't and won't happen if the 'spiritual' part of us is trying to keep the rest of us in order, but only if something from outside us draws every part of us, like a magnet, in the same direction. It is only if we respond with all that we are, heart and mind and body, to some force beyond ourselves which *claims* the whole of us that integration or wholeness can emerge. Now, of course, that force can be an evil force, and most of us are conscious of the evil effects a wholehearted response to a totalitarian political power or religion can bring. But the one and only unifying power which can draw together the scattered and divisive parts of ourselves is the magnetizing power of the God of Love. In the Old Testament, he is referred to as, 'I am that I am,' the one being who is wholly integrated. The measure of our response to the love of God is the measure of our wholeness and integration.

However, when we talk of the magnetizing *power* of the God of Love, we're not identifying that which is the dynamic and inspiration of goodness with power as is commonly understood. The contrast in the earthly life of Jesus between his utter powerlessness, and the power enthused about in popular religion, is striking. 'The God of Power', 'Healing by the Power of God', 'The Power of God in your everyday life': these phrases can woefully mislead, unless we're prepared to translate Power into Love, and see any assertion about the almightiness of God as being an assertion about the ultimate victory of love. This is hard to take, since for the best of motives, we want to ensure that Christian faith is seen as strong and effective in the world. And so we're tempted to keep a little bit of power in the wordly sense in reserve, whilst paying lip-service to the all-importance of love. Again, integration doesn't happen that way. We're refusing to take the full consequences of the vulnerability of love, and so are denying ourselves the real and ultimate strength which comes from such vulnerability. It was in the goodness combined with weakness displayed by Jesus on the cross, which impressed both the penitent thief: 'This man hath done nothing amiss' (Luke 23.41), and also the centurion: 'Truly this man was the Son of God' (Mark 15.39). And all this without a knowledge of the 'happy ending' which the resurrection guaranteed. The novelist Graham Greene illustrates this insight into the real nature of love's vulnerability when a character in his amusing novel *Monsieur Quixote*[1] points out what a different Christian faith we would now enjoy if Jesus had appealed to his Father in the Garden of Gethsemane to send more than twelve legions of angels – and they had actually arrived! And perhaps there's a part of us which wishes that they had, as a demonstration to convince the world of the power of God.

An intervening power from outside might have rescued Jesus in the Garden, or repressed the evil he was forced to endure. But, as Graham Shaw says,

> It could only have compromised his goodness, it could have added nothing to it. The disconcerting feature of his goodness is precisely that it has discarded all claim to power, human or divine; it does not need them. The man of God needs neither the violent defence of men nor the privileged intervention of an Almighty God – his goodness is quite independent of such support and alone sustains him in his weakness.[2]

Goodness as integration is the business of taking the consequences of the vulnerability and seeming powerlessness of love to its limits.

The magnetizing power of the God of love which holds us together often finds its expression in another outside ourselves – I mean, in our neighbour's need, the neighbour in whom we perceive the ever-present Christ. And his *real* need, not what we think would be good for him – and the needs, too, of those who do not parade them, but who suffer quietly and uncomplainingly. Again, contemplating the majestic power of love not only puts us in perspective, but enables us properly to *see* the other person, as he or she really is. All too often, we see other people in the light of our own reflection, or values or prejudices. To reflect to others that magnetic power is to work in selfless love for their welfare.

Incidentally, as with the individual, so with the church. When the church simply thinks about its own internal life and structures, or in terms of rules and spiritual direction, the life ebbs out of it. I learnt this lesson in my first experience with a Council of Churches in a Manchester parish. We only started to make progress in setting it up when we abandoned the task of sitting round listening to each other's story about our distinctive contribution to the universal church, and went about the business of two by two house-to-house collecting for Christian Aid. The 'going-out', not only in a literal sense, but also in the sense that we were serving in some small way the needs of humanity, brought a feeling of unity about which we had previously begun to despair.

How, then, does this goodness which is integration show itself? I take the example of someone who is trying to help another person, through counselling, formally or informally. Those of us who are in the middle of some personal crisis which is having a painful effect on our family, or health and ourselves feel that what we most need is someone to share the situation with us: someone who will help us to see things more clearly, and come to a mind about what action we should take. What sort of person would we most readily go to for this help? A genuine person, first: a person who wasn't wearing a mask, as it were, or hiding behind a professional barrier. Not, as we might say, a cold fish, seemingly disinterested in us or our situation, but a warm person, with whom you feel you could share the deepest secrets of your life without being subjected to criticism or judgment, and certainly without those secrets being betrayed, either implicitly or explicitly. A person, that is, who accepts you, without conditions, however grim the story you have to tell or however badly it reflects on you. Someone who will still value you as a person, or as the Americans say, 'prize you' as a parent 'prizes' a child, no matter what he or she may have done.

Henri Nouwen in his book with the characteristic title, *The Wounded Healer*, goes a little further, in suggesting that the task of the counsellor is 'to make one's own painful and joyful experiences available as sources of clarification and understanding':

Who can save a child from a burning house without taking the risk of being hurt by the flames? Who can listen to a story of loneliness and despair without taking the risk of experiencing similar pains in his own heart and even losing

47

his precious peace of mind? In short: who can take away suffering without entering it?[3]

So if you're going to enter into the sufferings of another person, to feel what the other person is feeling as if you were the other person, you're going to be stripped of all your pretensions, all the precious self-protections with which you usually face the world. I was both amused and encouraged the other day to hear a psychotherapist speak of his own discipline as that essentially of 'two nervous, frightened, anxious people sitting together in a consulting room ...' And how different that image is from that projected by earnest carers, or by professionals anxious, above all, to assert their own professional 'expertise'; different, too, from the presuppositions of many Christian people who presume that as the strong people we bring to others who are weak that which they need (or rather what we as Christians *think* they need!). Faith doesn't lie there; it lies in the sharing to the utmost point of weakness, without seeking refuge or self-protection. It's being with, at the bottom of the valley of the shadow – even of death. If, for instance, you're sitting at the bedside of a dying patient, it won't be so much as the helper, but as the one who is helpless (along with everyone else) to alter the situation, and yet as one whose honest admission of naked vulnerability is the only 'help'. I've always been moved by the strong phrase which St Paul uses in his letter to the Philippians in describing the way in which 'Christ Jesus, who being in the form of God, counted it not a prize to be on an equality with God, but emptied himself', (Phil. 1.6f.). That divine model of self-emptying points to the most valuable resource we possess in helping other people. I know that the times I've been of least help to other people have been those when I've been trying to get the other person to do what I thought best, subtly or not so subtly imposing my will on him or her.

That self-emptying in the light of the vision of God is, as we have seen, of the essence of goodness. But it is important to recollect what a strong phrase like that is saying. It isn't to indicate that we are to grovel, or feel that we have no worth or value, for clearly if we don't count ourselves to have value, there's no reason why we should count other people valuable either. We all have value, since we are each one of us made in the image of God (however defaced that image has become), the God who will never stop loving us whoever we are or whatever we do. The phrase 'naked vulnerability' which I have already used, is the phrase which to me most nearly describes in relation to ourselves the self-emptying of which St Paul speaks.

So how does this relate to integration? True self-emptying can only happen, it seems to me, if conflicts in ourselves have been largely resolved, and the warring factions we spoke of earlier have been drawn together by the magnetizing power of God's love. The force and inspiration of that love will make us lose much necessity for pretence, presumption or protection. And although we may reasonably hope that we are on the road to wholeness and integration, we shall be ready to acknowledge that there are things in our past which can never be undone; we shall be ready to accept the way in which we have been diminished by them. That doesn't necessarily spoil our integration, unless we use those things in some way to justify ourselves. The very limitation which any past may have imposed on us becomes part of our total self-giving, rather than some hindrance to it. For the integration of which we speak as goodness isn't simply synonymous with being 'psychologically well-adjusted' in the sense which the phrase is usually understood to convey: easy, amiable, going along with smoothly, always predictable. Just consider how Jesus would measure up to that standard: it was his very 'eccentricity', in the literal sense of the word, which led him to his cross. There are other grounds for 'being awkward' than psychological disturbance. And the haunting, luring quality of goodness will never allow us to be satisfied with easy predictability, or to rest complacent either with what we are, or with what we've done. Nor will it allow us to be diverted into what we imagine will be to our advantage, what is likely to be popular with other people, or win us favour.

One effect of the focussing of our attention on God and his goodness, drawing out from us an increasing wholeness, will be to give us constancy of purpose. It won't make us inflexible or dogmatic or unable to be self-critical: it will make us loyal to that truth which we have made our own, and for which in the end, we might be prepared to sacrifice our lives. As it has been said of Jesus, 'the truth he proclaimed, the truth by which he lived, the truth for which he died, was his own.'[4]

There are two well-known characters in history who have been portrayed in drama by Bernard Shaw and Robert Bolt, who display just this quality of goodness as integration, and so as integrity. After Joan of Arc signs a confession denying her voices, she finds out that she will be subjected to life imprisonment, and to be shut away from God's expression of love in his creation is to deny all that she is:

> Bread has no sorrow for me, and water no affliction. But to shut me from the light of the sky and the sight of the fields and flowers; to chain my feet so that I can never again ride with the soldiers nor climb the hills; to make me breathe foul damp darkness, and keep from me everything that brings me back to the love of God when your wickedness and foolishness tempt me to hate him: all this is worse than the furnace in the Bible that was heated seven times.[5]

Joan's integrity, her centring on God, finally demands that she recant and choose burning at the stake. And a century later than St Joan, Thomas More, the Man for All Seasons, facing a similar dilemma of conscience, as he languished in the Tower, is urged by his daughter Margaret to swear to the Act of Succession and so allow himself to be freed. She doesn't have much success.

When a man takes an oath, Meg, he's holding his own self in his hands. Like water ... And if he opens his fingers *then* – he needn't hope to find himself again.

Margaret then protests to him that he 'has done as much as God can reasonably want'. And that brings More to the heart of the matter.

Well ... finally ... it isn't a matter of reason; finally it's a matter of love.[6]

The wheel comes full circle. The more we are taken up by and absorbed in God's goodness and love, the more empty we shall be of any false self, the more whole and integrated we shall be as persons, the better we will be able to *see* and love and help our neighbours, the firmer we shall be in our integrity.

6

Goodness as Invisibility

How invisible are you? That isn't quite the stupid question it sounds, once we accept the primacy of contemplation. The continual looking towards God and his goodness endows us both with a sense of proportion about ourselves and with such confidence that we need not any longer try to make anything of ourselves, or even of what others think of us. We are secure in God's love for us. So we don't need any more to be continually noticed, or make others aware of our presence and assert ourselves. All that longing is properly satisfied in him.

Goodness and invisibility, then, are not all that far apart. This was bought home to me particularly by the novel by Iris Murdoch, called *The Nice and the Good*. It makes an important distinction: the nice are not necessarily the good, although we often too easily assume that they are. And the only person in the novel who approximates to the good is very much an off-centre character, old Uncle Theo, a man hardly crucial to the action of the book. He lives in a room, which he never allows anyone to clean, which smells of disinfectant and medicine and even more, of human sweat. And although the room is in a household teeming with people, he exists within a tiny circle of relationships, the best of which seems to be with Mingo, the dog. Most of the central characters in the novel ignore him, with the exception of Mary, who wonders about his invisibility, and whether it's due to his placidity of nature, or whether it's something he's actually achieved.

Uncle Theo puzzled Mary. She was also rather puzzled by the complete lack of curiosity about him evinced by other members of the household. The odd thing was that this lack of interest seemed to be caused in some positive way by Theo himself, as if he sent out rays which paralysed other people's concern and indeed Uncle Theo did often seem to have become almost imperceptible in a literal sense, as when someone said 'There was nobody there. Oh well, yes, Theo was there.'[1]

Near the end of the novel, it transpires that earlier in life, Theo had taken vows in a Buddhist monastery in search of a way of overcoming the relentless egotism of which he was so conscious in himself. But in the end he glimpses that the cost is too great.

Theo had begun to glimpse the distance which separates the nice from the good, and the vision of this gap had terrified his soul. He had seen, far off, what is perhaps the most dreadful thing in the world, the other face of love, its blank face. Everything that he was, even the best that he was, was connected with possessive self-filling human love. That blank demand implied the death of his whole being.[2]

Now towards the end of his life, and so without illusion and knowing full well his limitations, he decides to go back to the monastery.

Why should he stay here and rot? Perhaps the great mountain of himself would never grow less. But he could keep company with the enlightenment of others, and might regain at least the untempered innocence of a well-guarded child. And although he might never draw a single step closer to that great blankness he would know of its reality and feel more purely in the simplicity of his life the distant plucking of its magnetic power.[3]

And we are left wondering whether Theo will finally achieve that self-naughting, that complete invisibility which he knows to be his essential goal.

Another character who approximates to the good in Iris Murdoch's novels is that of Tallis in *A Fairly Honourable Defeat*.[4] He is both a lecturer in social sciences to WEA classes and a charitable social worker, and seems to be unremarkable at both jobs. Another character, Julius, refers to him as an 'unperson', and like Uncle Theo in *The Nice and the Good* he lives in squalor and smells. He seems to muddle along in life. Hilda thinks 'wherever Tallis is there's always muddle!' And she immediately realizes the injustice of that remark, and suggests that the reverse conveys the real truth about him: 'wherever there is muddle, there Tallis is.' Another clue to his character is given by Julius when he describes his tenacity: 'this dull holding on and hoping'. And at the end of the book, Tallis is shown still holding on, without self-deception. That makes him the least colourful, the least visible of all the characters in the novel: Morgan describes him as having 'no real conception of himself, there's a sort of emptiness'. But this strange invisibility goes alongside an ability to act spontaneously and decisively when events demand it. When a black man is being attacked by a gang of white thugs, and other onlookers dither, Tallis is the only one to act decisively by stepping forward and hitting the ring-leader with considerable force — and considerable effect. It is the same Tallis who forces the evil and conspiring Julius into a phone box to make a confession to Hilda of the way he had engineered events which have led to her husband's death. But apart from this capacity for quick and spontaneous action, when necessary, Tallis is a man who waits. He waits for his wife to end her affair, waits for her when she comes back to London, waits for Julius to confess, waits for his father to die. And his ability to wait without making things happen, without interfering, together with a quiet humble love which asks nothing for itself, but is ready to serve anyone who needs it: this is the goodness which makes him invisible.

In another of Iris Murdoch's novels, *The Unicorn*,[5] the character Effingham Cooper comes close to the experience of death as he sinks in a bog, and that experience opens his eyes for the first time: the blindness caused by his self-concern is removed. He realizes that what has slipped away from him is simply himself, and he realizes, too, that love is the business of looking and looking until the self doesn't exist any more – and it is a love which feels like death.

Invisibility, the death of the ego: isn't this the way in which goodness *shows* itself? Isn't this why some of those who have advanced furthest along the path to goodness are not necessarily those who have been canonized as saints or received any public notice at all, but those who have in some obscure corners of the earth, 'walked humbly with their God'? Donald Nicholl gives a dramatic illustration of this invisibility, which comes from north-east Tibet.[6] A very saintly man, well-known by pilgrims and the poor for his good works, was coming near to death, and made the request that his body should not be moved for a week. When he died his body was wrapped in old clothes and carried into a small room, by bearers who noticed that the old man appeared to have shrunk in size. Six days later, the family noticed that the body seemed to have shrunk still further. By the eighth day, when the time came for a burial, there was nothing left except the nails and the hair. The learned local Lama said that that experience was not uncommon and added that the body of the saintly man had been absorbed into the Light. His saintliness had made him invisible.

But how realistic is this invisibility? Does it not exclude the possibility of goodness from those who have to exercise authority and discipline? To put it bluntly, can a managing director or a Prime Minister afford to be invisible? There can, of course, be no absoluteness about this: like any other quality, it is a tendency, an emphasis, something that is always to some degree compromised. yet there are examples of those who in positions of power, have exercised such reticence and restraint and humility as to constitute near invisibility. The poisonous remarks made by the enemies of Clement Attlee when he was Prime Minister in the forties and fifties all relate to this particular quality, as indeed do the judgments of some historians that he was one of the wisest and best Prime Ministers of this century. John Harvey-Jones, for many years chairman of ICI, saw the company through a difficult phase in the seventies to come back in the eighties as one of Britain's most successful companies. You might think that to have done this, he had to display the qualities of ruthlessness and thrusting, a sort of managerial dictatorship. But recently he has written his reflections on leadership: *Making it Happen*. It is precisely the opposite of authoritarianism which he sees as the key to success. Rather, he believes that the key is the freedom given to the individual in the company, freedom to be honest about what needs to be done, freedom to participate in decision-making. There is a risk in this managerial invisibility, but it is a risk in his view which needs to be encouraged. He repeatedly says that 'people are self-motivated. They do their best work when they have come to believe, through their own processes, that what they are going to do is worthwhile. The free man is always better than the slave.'[7] He stresses that 'a vision is needed', but it is a vision which calls for 'more creativity and just straight humanity'. Obviously, I do not claim (any more than I could not claim!) that either Clement Attlee's seeming invisibility as a Prime Minister or John Harvey-Jones's as a managing director is due to their absorption in the magnetizing power of the love of God: I do claim that we might easily underestimate the practical effectiveness of goodness in tough, secular situations.

One way in which this invisibility displays itself in ordinary life goes back to the self-emptying of which we spoke in the last chapter when we were considering how best to help other people. For that self-emptying demands of us a precious surrender, perhaps the most precious surrender of all.

Suppose someone has enough trust and confidence in you as to enable them to talk to you about something they've done, something which stems from a completely different set of moral values from your own. If you simply remain who you are, and make moral judgments (implicitly or explicitly) about what they've done, then you won't only prevent yourself from helping: you will preclude any possibility of help in the future. You will, in short, slowly but firmly be shutting a door. In situations like this, we need to make great efforts to get out of our own skins, and assume theirs. That is, we need to see their actions in the way in which they see them, from the vantage-point of their own values, and that calls for a humility and self-emptying the like of which we rarely have to exercise in everyday life. It may feel like a painful betrayal of our best selves, and we can often justify our refusal 'to go that far' on the grounds that we shall be condoning what may be in our eyes, grossly offensive. But to be 'where they are' – even to those limits – is the most therapeutic resource we can ever offer, and it all stems from a willingness to become – invisible.

'I die daily,' said St Paul. But again, we're not talking about the deliberate act of self-sacrifice in order to achieve this invisibility. That might lead us back to concentrate on ourselves – martyrs have often been accused of a higher selfishness! It's the attention, the looking, which achieves silently and naturally this invisibility.

But, of course, there are a few occasions in life when a choice has to be made in dramatic circumstances. Mother Maria was a Russian nun presiding over a convent in Paris in 1940. When the Germans occupied the city, she told her chaplain that she felt she must give all possible assistance to persecuted Jews. She realized it would mean imprisonment and possibly death, and although she gave him the option of leaving, the chaplain decided to stay. So Mother Maria hid women and children within the convent for a month, and hundreds of them were enabled to escape from France.

Then, at the end of the month, the Gestapo came. Mother Maria was arrested, and sent to the concentration camp at Ravensbruck. Her chaplain was sent to Buchenwald, and there he died of starvation and overwork. Mother Maria, or 'that wonderful Russian nun', as she was known even to the guards, had been in the camp two-and-a-half years when a new block of buildings was erected in the camp, and the prisoners, as usual, were told that these were to be hot baths. The day came when a few dozen prisoners from the women's quarters were lined up outside the buildings. When one girl became hysterical, Mother Maria, who had not been selected (indeed, it seems doubtful whether the Germans had any intention of killing her) came up to her. 'Don't be frightened,' she said. 'Look, I shall take your turn,' and in line with the rest, she passed through the doors. The date was Good Friday, 1945.[8]

Such an action could only be seen by the world as divine madness in the same sense in which 'the word of the cross is unto them that are perishing foolishness; but unto us which are being saved, it is the power of God' (I Cor. 1.18). Christ crucified is 'unto Jews a stumbling-block, and unto Gentiles foolishness', but there are those with eyes to see that this is both 'the power of God, and the wisdom of God'. But in order to see that, we must contemplate 'the wondrous cross' and so be taken up by 'love so amazing, so divine' that we penetrate a little closer to the heart of goodness, and become somewhat transformed by it. And that could mean that we shall be a little more – invisible.

7

Nurturing Goodness: In the Church

How are we, in today's world, to begin to demonstrate our concern for goodness – and further, begin to nurture goodness? In one way, the time is ripe. There has been a growing demand recently by politicians for a social cohesion born of individual morality and responsibility, and this plea is in tune with a growing popular unease in the country generally about social evils like rising crime statistics. Of course, politicians often make statements about morality for purely political ends, but often their insistence on the necessity for individual morality highlights what has become a slightly distorted emphasis in recent presentation of the gospel at a public level. No one could rightly dispute that that gospel has severe social and political implications in 'bias to the poor' and a care for the underprivileged in society. But we need to recognize that even if all those implications were taken care of, the most fundamental question of all for Christian faith, and (I would add) for society at large, is how do we help fashion human beings to the full point of their humanity? How do we foster that maturity, that morality which may 'keep the rules' but which also goes far beyond them, and implies living which is creative and spontaneous? How, in other words, can we instil the desire for goodness in people?

We live in an era when the church is declining in many fields. For several years, there has been a steady fall in the number of baptisms, confirmations, Easter communicants, ordinations, church marriages and electoral roll membership. And whilst some of this decline may signal 'a healthy stripping down for action', as it has been called, the direction that action seems to be taking is a bizarre response to the spiritual vacuum in which millions of people live their lives. If the work of the Church of England General Synod is to be taken as any sort of yardstick as to the church's main preoccupations, then its primary responsibility to develop and nurture Christian formation and sanctification rates a very low priority indeed. It has dissipated (in the literal sense of the word) its energy on all sorts of social causes, which however admirable in themselves, have given the impression, at least, that social and political commitment by Christians is both more important and relevant than striving for individual Christian discipleship. Of course, all Christian discipleship bears within it the seeds of political and social commitment. But that commitment comes as the fruit of a developing Christian life which is seen as an end in itself – and on that sort of individual growth and formation the church is remarkably silent.

Hardly less than a revolution is necessary in the ordering of church life and its priorities. It would scarcely have been possible for someone who was seriously and honestly searching for an answer to the question, 'What does Christian faith have to offer me if I want to live my life well?' to have found any convincing answer if he simply looked at what, for instance, our 'quality' newspapers were reporting about the Anglican church over the past four or five years. He would gain the impression of doctrinal chaos, with bishop fighting bishop over empty tombs, personal animosities fuelled by the Crockford affair, and obsession with institutional issues like the ordination or women and the question of homosexual clergy. Granted that all these issues were just the sort of issues a hungry press was searching for, I have to say that the impression wouldn't be far from the truth. The image projected by the church is that of a club or pressure-group with an agenda, rather than of a community in Christ, encouraging and stimulating individuals to that 'mature manhood, measured by nothing less than the full stature of Christ' (Eph. 4.13).

Let me illustrate what I mean. One central proposition to which Christians of almost any persuasion would assent to would surely be that 'God is unconditional love, and this love is seen supremely in Jesus Christ.' (If the word 'God' were a stumbling-block for some, then we might substitute 'At the heart of the universe there is unconditional love.') There is enough 'agenda' in the depth of that simple statement to last the church for years – if it is willing to meditate on it, and act on all its profound implications. But would our honest enquirer believe for a moment when he or she then reads news of the church that that was our fundamental concern? Of course, if they go to church, they will encounter some loving individuals; but would they feel caught up in, and hope to be transformed by a community which is giving itself away for the sake of others?

I have been re-reading recently the classic *Letters and Papers from Prison* of Dietrich Bonhoeffer, and found myself both excited and depressed at what I was reading. Excited, because in his writing he again and again touches nerve-ends, and you feel the truth of what he is saying about Christ and the church – and his imprisonments and martyrdom puts the seal of veracity on it all. Depressed, because despite all that has been written about him, all the publicity he has been given in drama, documentaries and the like, you feel the total effect of his prophecy on the life of the church forty years later has been minimal. Take, for instance, his statement that 'the church is the church only when it exists for others'. He pleads that to make a start, it should give away all its property to those in need, an illustration of the way its calling is to help and serve men, and not lord it over them or be caught up in the vices of 'power-worship, envy, and humbug'. Above all, he stresses 'the importance of human example (which has its origin in the humanity of Jesus and is so important in Paul's teaching); it is not abstract argument, but example that gives its word emphasis and power'.[1] Surely it is ironic that the most dramatic examples of giving to the poor

63

and needy and helping and serving others have not come
from the church in recent years, but from the intricate and
united efforts of pop-groups and comedians, in Band-Aid and
Comic Relief. I don't say this grudgingly: the Spirit of God
fills the world, as well as the church. But it seems to me to
highlight the distorted perspective and priorities which the
church still possesses, despite all the prophecies of people like
Bonhoeffer.

If the growth in goodness is ever to receive its due weight in
the life of the church, then we must give more consideration
to the interior life of the Christian, give more time to personal
direction and interior disciplines. Traditionally, wherever
activities like corporate meditation or silence have been tried
in the local church, they have been badly supported, especially
by men, with Bible-reading only slightly less badly because
presumably there is something rather more 'down to earth'
about that. ('After all, it's concerned with behaviour and
morality, isn't it?') I am convinced that the climate is
changing, that those so-called 'spiritual' activities are increasingly seen to be necessary, and that if we go on neglecting
them, we shall find out (as has happened time and time again)
that the secular world will have once more stolen a march on
us. Recently, I have been overwhelmed by the popular
response to different series of hour-long meditations which I
have been responsible for writing and presenting on the ITV
network on Sunday morning. These are transmitted in place
of the traditional outside-broadcast service of worship. In the
meditations I spoke as person-to-person, and we deliberately
dealt with personal themes such as guilt, failure, good
and bad memories and hope. I have explored these themes by
means of exposition of the psychological and theological
dimensions involved, interviews with those whom the particular theme has touched, or is touching deeply, music, secular
and Bible reading, appropriate hymns (with the words chosen
very carefully to illustrate the theme) prayer – and above all,
silence. (An illustration of the fact that silence has been

ignored in religious television was the way in which we had to warn transmitter-operations, lest they should think that something was wrong!) So many people who phoned and wrote after the broadcasts explained how they felt as if they were personally helped in their spiritual pilgrimage – and far more so than if they just experienced what many of them called the 'coldness' and the 'impersonality' of a church service. Now, of course, it's easy to exaggerate the importance of something in which you have been personally and deeply involved, but I have been left convinced that we should stimulate the quiet, meditative, contemplative gift in as many ways as possible: through group 'awareness' exercises in the open air, through an increasing use of silence in church worship, through encouragement to individual exercises in contemplation, through specific teaching on simple methods of meditation. (Again, on this latter point, I was staggered by the number of requests we received after the TV broadcast for an elementary leaflet I had drawn up on such methods for people with very different backgrounds.) I have insisted elsewhere[2] that in the common life of the church we pay insufficient attention to adult Christian education, for which a better word might be 'formation'. For when such education is divorced from notions of information and factual know-ledge ('What were the dimensions of Solomon's temple?' 'Trace the different routes covered by St Paul in his three missionary journeys') it encourages such formation through the process of clarification, honest enquiry and self-exposure in a supportive and loving atmosphere. It is my own parti-cular experience over twenty years which prompts me to say that the rewards given to an adult educator in terms of seeing results in the lives of those whom he teaches are often considerable, and leads me to think that if only we would afford it a much higher priority, then we should find the life of the church increasingly transformed.

Above all, the nurture of goodness in others depends on the way in which we develop in our own personal lives the

8

Nurturing Goodness: The Experience of C. S. Lewis

'A non-playing captain in the game of love and grief suddenly called in to play.' So one TV critic described C. S. Lewis, in reviewing the programme *Shadowlands*, which tells the story of his love for Joy Davidman, her subsequent death through cancer shortly after their marriage, and his reaction to it. The critic might have added that when Lewis took his turn at the crease, he found it to be a very different game in the middle from that which he had coolly contemplated, enthusiastically studied and so logically theorized about from the pavilion.

In his book, *Christian Behaviour*, written in 1943, Lewis had been able to view with detachment the business of falling in love. A notion that we get from novels and plays, he says, is that 'falling in love' is quite irresistible: 'something that happens to one, like measles'.[1] And then he went on to argue that whilst we ought to admire the qualities of someone beautiful and clever and sympathetic, it is in our own choice whether this admiration turns into 'being in love'. 'That will be our own fault,' he harshly concludes. In the same chapter, Lewis is equally harsh on the subject of divorce, on which he says the churches are all agreed that 'it is more like having both your legs cut off than it is like dissolving a business partnership or even deserting a regiment. What they all disagree with is the modern view that it is a simple readjustment of partners, to be made whenever people feel they are no longer in love with one another, or when either of them falls in love with someone else.'[2]

Similarly, three years earlier, Lewis was able to write serenely of pain and suffering:

> I have seen great beauty of spirit in some who were great sufferers. I have seen men, for the most part, grow better not worse with advancing years, and I have seen the last illness produce treasures of fortitude and meekness from uncompromising subjects. I see in loved and revered historical figures, such as Johnson and Cowper, traits which might scarcely have been tolerable if the man had been happier. If the world is indeed 'a vale of soul-making', it seems on the whole to be doing its work.[3]

And of death, and its sequel, which he compares to a dance.

> There is joy in the dance, but it does not exist for the sake of joy. It does not even exist for the sake of good, or of love. It is Love Himself and *Good* Himself, and therefore happy. It does not exist for us, but we wait for it.[4]

It was bitterly ironic that each of these human experiences about which Lewis so confidently wrote beforehand, he later underwent. He met Joy Davidman in 1952 and fell in love with her. He described how for a few years they 'feasted on love; every mode of it – solemn and merry, romantic and realistic, sometimes as dramatic as a thunderstorm, sometimes as comfortable and unemphatic as putting on your soft slippers. No cranny of heart or body remained unsatisfied.'[5] It was said of them that 'there were never two people alive in the history of the world who were more in love than Jack and Joy'. Having had that experience, could Lewis then glibly have said that what had happened was his own choice, or even more his own *fault*? But Joy was divorced from her husband Bill – and it is probable that their relationship would never have developed had it not been for Joy's unhappy marriage: her contact with Lewis through their letters seems to have made her long for liberation from the oppressive marriage-bond. Could he ever again have seen divorce in such coldly clinical or abstract terms as he did in *Christian Behaviour*? 'A simple readjustment of partners' was a ludicrously inadequate description of what happened to them both. And then of her pain and suffering and death and his honest reaction Lewis writes in *A Grief Observed*:

> Where is God? Go to Him when your need is desperate, when all other help is vain, and what do you find? A door slammed in your face, and a sound of bolting and double-bolting on the inside. After that, silence. You may as well turn away. The longer you wait, the more emphatic the silence will become.[6]

Through all these experiences, what had been so clear and self-evident before in the light of his neatly tied-and-packaged Christian faith now became confused areas of questioning and doubt. Once he allows his 'red-hot memory' to play on these experiences, he confesses that 'all this commonsense vanishes like an ant in the mouth of a furnace'. And he comes to the conclusion that his has been 'an imaginary faith playing with innocuous counters labelled "Illness", "Pain", "Death" and "Loneliness"'.

C. S. Lewis made a great contribution both to twentieth-century Christian thought and to the strengthening of the faith of individual Christians, especially in the difficult times of the Second World War and its aftermath. I, for one, had every reason to be grateful to him and his writings during my war-time service. Amidst all the questionings and the spiritual turmoil that were involved in attempting to put together the Christian faith and the bestiality of war, Lewis, an intelligent and scholarly layman, stood out as an apostle of conviction and faith. And, of course, it's true that Lewis was able before his death to come through to some reconciliation between his faith and his personal experience of tragedy. In his last work, *Letters to Malcolm*, he made it clear that he felt that although he was still surrounded by darkness, he shared that darkness both with Malcolm and 'with our Master'.

> ... Out of this evil comes a good. If I never fled from his presence, then I should suspect those moments when I seemed to delight in it of being wish-fulfilment dreams. That, by the way, explains the feebleness of all those watered versions of Christianity which leave out all the darker elements and try to establish a religion of pure consolation.
>
> No real belief in the watered versions can last.[7]

What happened in the life of C. S. Lewis is very relevant to the nurture of a spirituality and goodness related to real human experience. It seems as if we still neglect to take the depths of human experience and emotion seriously and attempts to relate it (however untidily) to Christian faith. And this in some sense is to turn our backs on the implications of the incarnation, possibly because it is too threatening and disturbing.

It was said of C. S. Lewis that 'he was so well defended against emotion that it seems sometimes he was encased in an armour only suitable for tilting and jousting in a cosy fairyland with his J. R. R. Tolkein'. It was the force of emotion breaking through at different levels which shattered the invulnerable shell of dogmatic theology with which Lewis had protected himself: no longer could he live in that 'cosy fairyland'. (Incidentally, that isn't a bad description of the way in which those outside the church sometimes see the realm we inhabit.) So there was a double tragedy in the expression of his faith: his invulnerability which left him quite unprepared when he had to relate the force of what was going on inside him with his Christian faith and the shortness of time he was given after he had lived through those experiences to make a greater contribution of a mature faith which emerged from his double reflection on his beliefs and on his experience.

The experience of C. S. Lewis for which adherence to the neat formulations of Christian theology had totally unprepared him poses a piercing question for those of us concerned with a search for goodness. How does goodness show itself in the most tender, poignant or bitter moments of our lives? Suppose my husband has walked out on me and left me to struggle with four children; suppose I am suffering from an inoperable cancer; suppose I am the victim of a clinical depression due to a chemical imbalance, and consequently over which I have no rational control; suppose I am bereaved and a widower at the age of forty-five, and facing a vacuum of loneliness which seemingly stretches endlessly into the future? Wherein, then, does goodness consist? Clearly, of course, there are no blanket responses that can rightly be made to any of these situations; each can only sensitively be dealt with by the wisdom of any pastor involved in them. But my point is that it is about the wrestling with such situations that we need to be concerned – and all too often there is little evidence of such concern.

There is only one branch of theology which could bridge the gap between what have become the abstractions of doctrinal formulae (it is sometimes difficult to believe that they all originated in human experience) and where men and women *really* are, what they go through, experience and of which they try to make sense. And that branch, pastoral theology, is sadly the most neglected of all. Where in academic theological circles its existence is even recognized, it is hardly more than patronized in a climate where social theology *appears* to have more relevance, where 'issues of contemporary significance' seem more exciting to the academic but often seem light-years away from where ordinary mortals struggle in their everyday existence. (I except universities north of the Border, with their admirable emphasis on 'practical theology', from these strictures.) There has never been a better time in which to do pastoral theology, for there are open to us now all the insights which have been developed in the human sciences over the past fifty years. And the challenging and exciting task ahead is to see what light these insights throw, for instance, on our Christian doctrine of man, and so help us to make *real* and not text-book responses to *real* situations and offer *real* guidance in man's search for goodness. And sometimes pastoral theology is its own worst enemy, dissipating its energies in the incestuous exercise of trying to prove conceptually that it is worthy of academic credibility, forgetting that its real credibility will only emerge in so far as it is seen to have a real impact on the lives of 'ordinary' men and women, encouraging and feeding them in their pilgrimage to goodness.

The result of this neglect is self-evident to those who dare to look. Many laypeople have deserted the church after years of struggle with what they know to be its massive irrelevance to their ordinary lives, its existence in a 'cosy fairyland'. We must surely learn the lesson posed so painfully by the life of C. S. Lewis, if we are to offer any stimulus in the life of goodness. We must cease to run away from exploring the depths of human experience, become humble enough to learn from secular disciplines more about these experiences, and integrate what it discovers in the face it presents to the world. Unless and until, that is, we begin to take pastoral theology seriously, we shall fail to find credibility amongst those who still wistfully turn to us for guidance – and what is more, we will not deserve to.

Pope John Paul II set us all a task when, speaking to the European bishops in October 1985, he said, 'we need heralds of the gospel who are experts in humanity, who have penetrated the depths of the human heart, who have shared to the full their joys and hopes, the anguish and sadness of our day, but who are at the same time, contemplatives in love with God.' In our search for goodness, our contemplation is directed heavenwards; but our feet are firmly planted in the earthiness of our daily experiences.

9

Nurturing Goodness: In the Young

Recently, a group of highly articulate young people voiced their sentiments, during the course of a Thames TV programme, *Tomorrow Talking*, about what matters in life. Their honesty was commendable, even if their ruthlessness was deeply disturbing. They were quite clear that success must be pursued at all costs, and that that would mean pushing other people aside, having no consideration for their feelings, for if you want to get on, you must concentrate simply and solely on number one.

Whilst these views are obviously not universally true of young people today (and many are better than their provocative words allow) the picture has a sufficient ring of truth about it as to highlight the contrast between what they're saying and all that we have been exploring in terms of goodness. The chasm seems unbridgeable. How has it come about that the 'current pantheon of heroes' is full not of those whose aim in life has been service and devotion to humanity, but of those who are self-centred, self-made achievers? Is it, as Anthony Clare suggests, because 'an undiluted media diet of fictional Rambos and factual Oliver Norths has totally bewitched our impressionable young'?

May it not also be in consequence of our current educational emphasis on the functional and the technical and the desire above all to get quick results, rather than the noble traditional view that education is an end in itself? What is clear is that both education and society itself have generally failed to inspire in our young people any vision beyond this one immediate and selfish end: a vision of a more just and fair society for all, and a vision of themselves as anything other than uncompromising egotists!

Iris Murdoch has written that 'a man's morality is not only his choices, but his vision'. One of the distressing features of the contemporary confusion about religious and moral education is the way in which little space seems to be given to the importance of stimulating vision in children and adolescents, encouraging them to explore models who will be for them in the future inspirations and examples. As we mentioned earlier, figures like Albert Schweitzer, David Livingstone and the like were common currency twenty-five or thirty years ago – even if the feet of clay which some of them possessed were kept discreetly hidden! Where are such models now? Exploration of topical ethical issues such as abortion and euthanasia, the use of drugs, peace and violence can only take your minds and spirits so far. If the challenge of goodness and the excitement of its pursuit is not also presented to them, the debate about ethical issues will become sterile and profitless, a mathematical juggling with arguments, lacking an overarching goal or theme.

So how is that challenge to be presented? Earnest moralists and politicians press for firm teaching of 'traditional moral values'. But the trouble with their approach is their desire for quick results – natural in the politicans, since in other areas of life with which they are concerned, it is only necessary to secure the legislation, and the deed will be done. They seem to forget that old adage that 'you can't make people good by Act of Parliament,' or even by using a lot of media publicity in order to press upon them its necessity. Exhortations like those of the four-year-old John Ruskin, 'People, be good,' don't work, for a whole variety of reasons. Growth in goodness is slow, indirect, oblique. It can't directly be taught: consider the way in which attempts to frame a coherent moral education syllabus, seen not long ago as the answer to our problems, have largely been abandoned. Appeals to the church, seen in the popular mind as the self-styled guardian of morality, to inculcate moral standards of right and wrong are bound to fail in the short term, and in any case always beg the question of the relativity, the greyness of the greater majority of our moral decisions. Goodness only grows with the sustained practice of our faith, and especially with the practice of those interior disciplines in which our lives are hidden with Christ-in-God. There is one obvious pragmatic truth which should be written on the heart of all would-be moral educators: you only exert influence in so far as you are not trying to exert any influence at all. The extent to which you're keen to influence someone in a certain moral direction (unless the other person is weak, and simply ready to be manipulated) is the extent to which you will have little or no influence. Those of us who are parents, for instance, will have learnt painfully over a long period of time that whilst our children seem wilfully to refuse to heed all our intense exhortations, they will imitate behaviour they see in us, and often when it's the last thing we want them to see. But somehow, we refuse to take to heart the implication of this simple pragmatic truth in order to encourage the growth of goodness. It is linked with another fact of my own experience and, I believe, of other people as well. The dawning of goodness in us has been a response to the goodness we have seen in others. Our moments of greatest clarity and enlightenment have come when we have seen something in them which we dimly recognize to be the pearl of great price for which we would consider many other things in the world to be well lost. How many times have we had the experience of being told by someone we've known many years previously that some incident in which we've been involved, or some remark we've made has been a significant landmark in that person's development – even though we were unconscious of it at the time, and have probably forgotten it ever since!

Those who are most vociferous in their demands for a return to 'Victorian values' or what they consider to be moral absolutes don't realize for a moment how sentimental or unrealistic they are in their demands. Likewise, those who call for more severe and sometimes vicious punishment for those convicted of particular crimes and believe that this will of itself lead to their reformation of character make the same facile mistake. Their sentimentality prevents them from going to the root of the matter and asking how any of us come to a recognition of moral values, preparing to make those values our own. (Perhaps because the real answer is of a slow, patient and quiet character, and not something which corresponds to the noise and vociferous nature of their demands?) In days when all authority is suspect – especially that which is claimed by right, rather than earned – it is surely plain, in the words of George Herbert that 'the fire in the flint shows not till it be struck'. But that fire is not struck unless and until we are with someone who is not intent on striking that fire, but is the sort of person with whom we can identify, and so who strikes the fire almost without noticing it.

Consider how important fairy-tales are in our moral development, and what we learn from them about moral development in general. Bruno Bettelheim spent a year in the concentration camps of Dachau and Buchenwald, and later became Professor of Psychology and Psychiatry at the University of Chicago. His chief interest has been that of working with disturbed children. He is quite clear about how our moral development happens.

It is not the fact that virtue wins out at the end which promotes morality, but that the hero is most attractive to the child, who identifies with the hero in all his struggles. Because of this identification the child imagines that he suffers with the hero his trials and tribulations, and triumphs with him as virtue is victorious. The child makes such identifications all on his own, and the inner and outer struggles of the hero imprint morality on him ... A child's choices are based not so much on right versus wrong, as on who arouses his sympathy and who his antipathy. The more simple and straightforward a good character, the easier it is for a child to identify with it and to reject the bad other. The child identifies with the good hero not because of his goodness, but because the hero's condition makes a deep positive appeal to him. The question for the child is not 'Do I want to be good?' but 'Who do I want to be like?' The child decides this on the basis of projecting himself whole-heartedly into one character. If this fairy-tale figure is a very good person, then the child decides that he wants to be good, too.[1]

But children need more than fairy-tales, however important they are: they also need living examples of men and women who carry around with them and in them the mystery and luminosity of goodness. And perhaps the tragedy is that the pop-stars and sportsmen of whom they hear most today are (with a few honourable exceptions) part of the contemporary cult of toughness, brashness and self-dominance, or in other words, a denial of those qualities which we associate with goodness. And unless the child is fortunate enough to have formed relationships with adults such as, for instance, teachers, living examples of the mystery and power of goodness, then what good memory is he or she likely to carry over into adult life? In Dostoevsky's novel, *The Brothers Karamazov*. Alyosha says to the boys gathered at Ilyusha's stone:

> My dear children ... you must know that there is nothing higher and stronger and more wholesome and good for life in the future than some good memory, especially a memory of childhood. People talk to you a great deal about your education, but some good, sacred memory, preserved from childhood, is perhaps the best education. If a man carried many such memories with him into life he is safe to the end of his days, and if one has only good memory left in one's heart, even that may be the means of saving us.

Exploration into Goodness

All this is well illustrated by the moral educator who insisted that schoolboys were more likely to 'catch' their moral development from the schoolmaster with whom they went canoeing out of school hours, and experienced all the hazards and the way in which the master faced and overcame those hazards, than they were from any moral education class in school. I happen to think that part of that secret was that it was out of school hours, without any compulsion on the master to be with the boys: the surrendering of his free time, the going over and beyond what duty demanded, for their sake – that sort of gesture has an incalculable effect, as I can testify myself. One of the schoolmasters to whom I owe most was one who gave two or three hours a week after school to coach two of us for university scholarships.

Perhaps one of the saddest features of life in the church over the past two or three decades has been the increasing lack of contact with children and young people. There was always much about the old Sunday school system – as I knew it, for instance, in Lancashire, where it was stronger than almost anywhere else in the country – which was totally inadequate, judged by modern educational theory and practice. But it enshrined one principle of inestimable value: it provided a place of friendship between caring adults and children, and especially for those children who came from broken or deprived homes. And friendship is the operative word. Time and time again I find the person and 'what the person was' remembered, when every scrap of teaching seems to have gone. Someone I remember described all clubs for young people as being 'organized friendship', especially where the clubs are small and domestic enough for there to arise quite naturally and spontaneously a warm relationship between the leader and the members. This sounds, I know, as if I am nostalgically pleading for a return to the old days, when things were better. Not so. I'm suggesting that, in circumstances where numbers have diminished, we have a chance to develop golden opportunities in small groups of just such 'organized friendship'. If these opportunities are presented to caring lay people as the most realistic contribution they can make both to helping children and young people grow up well, and to the health of society in general, I am confident that there would be a sufficient response. The form of activity – canoeing, doing up an old person's flat or garden, a sponsored swim – doesn't matter. It is the friendship which counts providing, as always, it is unconditional, that is, done for its own sake and out of genuine love for others, rather than to satisfy some need in the carer to witness to the gospel, or to increase numbers at church, the subtlest manipulation of all.

Now what does all this mean in practice? First, it means that we shall not be satisfied with a negative approach to the quest for goodness, an approach which is content to make everything relative, to minimize or to debunk. Ever since Lytton Strachey's *Eminent Victorians*, there has been an insidious desire to dethrone the eminent, find the worm in the apple, and make the famous appear to be ordinary people, 'just like us...' But the 'warts and all' approach, whilst representing a healthy reaction against the over-adulatory approach of some earlier biography, can be equally deformative of the truth about a character, for in its concentration on 'flaws', it can fail to recognize the commitment of the character to that which lay beyond himself, and his stumbling pilgrimage towards its embodiment. And as we have already seen, when did goodness simply imply moral excellence? Constant exposure to such debunking, and playing down of the good can only lead to cynicism, and at a time of life when adolescence is naturally pointing in the direction of idealism, can spoil and possibly harm for good those aspirations towards goodness. The person who has convinced himself that his fellow-creatures are all second-rate is content as a rule to be second-rate himself.

Secondly, it means that we shall recognize and act upon ways in which goodness is caught and not taught in a thousand 'minute particulars'. In school, and indeed in church, it will be through the way in which people look at one another, speak to one another, listen to one another, the stress on courtesy: it will be the way in which achievement is adequately credited and appreciated, without belittling or despising those who are decreed to have failed, the way in which every child, however backward, is deemed valuable ... So there will be no sense in which whatever is being directly taught by way of religious or moral education will be indirectly denied by assumption and practice in school or church itself. And if the essential vision is going to be caught, it will only be through the individual lives of those with whom the child is daily in contact, whose who quite unself-consciously communicate their own vision.

That vision isn't just a vision of ourselves as we would like to be: it is a vision of ourselves as we were meant to be. And that implies a vision of God and his goodness, and the love that flows from and exemplifies that vision. In so far as we give ourselves to those with whom we come into touch, as our faint response to God's love, something of that love will be seen, heard and felt by them, and they will receive something of the vision that we have experienced.

Epilogue

We began our exploration into goodness by looking at its attractiveness; its haunting, dream-like appearance, even in the worst of circumstances. That dream persists even in days like these, when evil almost seems to reach saturation-point with us. But goodness doesn't only attract; paradoxically, it can repel, too. In the presence of goodness, we find our hidden and suspicious motives exposed, our dark side brought into an uncomfortable light, our unworthiness shown up by the sheer power of its opposite. And we may not only find it unacceptable. We may come to hate the goodness, and worse still, the embodying of that goodness.

The twentieth-century musician, Arnold Schoenberg, considers the composer Gustav Mahler to have been a saint, and expected that everyone who knew him, even slightly, would share that judgment. But he told how only a few men of good will really honoured Mahler.

> The others reacted to the saint as evil has always reacted to goodness and greatness: they martyred him. They carried things so far that this good man doubted his own work. Not once was the cup allowed to pass away from him. Even the bitterest he had to drink: the loss, if only temporary, of faith in his work.[1]

The allusion to the cup is timely, for it takes us back to the Garden of Gethsemane, where Jesus faced the agony of reward for his goodness engendered in the ruling powers. Whatever the love of goodness, the pilgrimage towards it is often as hard as the wood and nails of the cross of Christ.

But our faith is not in ourselves, or in our goodness, but in God, the source of all goodness. Genesis tells us that God saw everything that he had made, and behold it was very good. That means that there is a fundamental goodness in creation, so well-rooted that no evil can in the end blot it out; because always, no matter what happens, good will surface once more. And of that truth, the resurrection is the guarantee. Whatever the appearances, whatever its seeming defect, goodness is writ in the heavens, for eternity. And its power on earth will never finally be extinguished.

There shall never be one lost good!
What was, shall live as before;
The evil is null, is nought, is silence implying sound;
What was good, shall be good, with, for evil, so much good more;
On the earth the broken arcs; in the heaven, a perfect round.[2]

On the earth, we learn to live with the 'broken arcs' – and there, often, lies our difficulty. We long for completeness, definiteness, certitude, all of which true faith will deny us. It is for us so to live close to the source of all goodness that we are able to perceive 'broken arcs' of that goodness in the most unlikely people and places, able to coax out of the most unprofitable soil some tender (if sometimes colourful!) plants. For we will recognize them as signs and symbols pointing to that 'distant, transcendent Perfection', that Vision of God, which is our constant encouragement and hope.

Notes

Prologue

1. Donald Nicholl, *Holiness*, Darton, Longman and Todd 1981; and Philip Sheldrake, *Images of Holiness*, Darton, Longman and Todd 1987.

1 · The Attraction of Goodness

1. Mary Midgley, *Wickedness*, Ark 1986.
2. Quoted by Malcolm Muggeridge, *Christ and the Media*, Hodder and Stoughton 1977, p. 46.
3. Monica Furlong, *Thérèse of Lisieux*, Virago 1987.
4. Dennis Potter, *Sufficient Carbohydrate*, Faber and Faber 1983, pp. 12f.
5. Alistair Cooke, *Six Men*, Bodley Head 1987, p. 179.
6. Anthony Trollope, *Barchester Towers*, 1857; Everyman edn 1941, p. 462.
7. *The Collected Poems of Stevie Smith*, Penguin Modern Classics 1985, p. 328. Used by permission.
8. Oldsey and Weintraub, *The Art of William Golding*, Indiana University Press 1968, p. 24.
9. Albert Camus, *The Plague*, Penguin 1960, p. 208.
10. Iris Murdoch, *The Good Apprentice*, Chatto and Windus 1985; Penguin edn, p. 55.
11. Ibid., p. 52.
12. Ibid., p. 53.
13. Primo Levi, *Moments of Reprieve*, Sphere Books 1987, p. 155.
14. Myra Schneider, *Fistful of Yellow Hope*, Littlewood Press 1984, p. 8.
15. Richard Mackenna, *Is There Anyone There?* Collins 1987, p. 97.

2 · The Vision of God and Goodness

1. Iris Murdoch, *The Sovereignty of Good*, Routledge and Keagan Paul 1970, p. 101.

2. John A. T. Robinson, *Where Three Ways Meet*, SCM Press 1987, p. 136.

3. Ibid., p. 191.

4. Iris Murdoch, op. cit., pp. 103–4.

5. Harry Williams, *Tensions*, Mitchell Beazley 1976, pp. 111, 113.

6. Clifford Longley, 'The Inward Calm of Holiness', article in *The Times*, 26 April 1988.

7. Nicholas of Cusa, *The Vision of God*.

8. Clifford Longley, art. cit.

3 · Spontaneous Goodness

1. Harry Williams, *True Resurrection*, Mitchell Beazley 1972, pp. 114, 115.

2. Ibid., p. 125.

3. Donald Nicholl, *Holiness*, Darton, Longman and Todd 1981, p. 150.

4 · Goodness as Loving

1. Viktor Frankl, *The Doctor and the Soul*, Penguin 1973, p. 134.

2. Frank Wright, *Pastoral Care for Lay People*, SCM Press 1982, p. 44.

3. C. S. Lewis, *The Four Loves*, Geoffrey Bles 1960.

5 · Goodness as Integration

1. Graham Greene, *Monsieur Quixote*, Bodley Head 1982.

2. Graham Shaw, *God in Our Hands*, SCM Press 1987, p. 124.

3. Henri Nouwen, *The Wounded Healer*, Doubleday 1972, pp. 72–73.

4. Harry Williams, *The True Wilderness*, Constable 1965, p. 159.

5. G. B. Shaw, *Saint Joan*, Scene VI.

6. Robert Bolt, *A Man for All Seasons*, Heinemann 1960, Act II.

6 · Goodness as Invisibility

1. Iris Murdoch, *The Nice and the Good*, Chatto and Windus 1968; Penguin 1969, p. 89.

2. Ibid., pp. 359–60.

3. Ibid., p. 361.

4. Iris Murdoch, *A Fairly Honourable Defeat*, Chatto and Windus 1970.

5. Iris Murdoch, *The Unicorn*, Chatto and Windus 1963.

6. Donald Nicholl, *Holiness*, Darton, Longman and Todd 1981, p. 22.

7. John Harvey-Jones, *Making it Happen*, Collins 1988, p. 260.

8. Victor Gollancz (ed), *A Year of Grace*, Gollancz 1950, p. 209.

7 · Nurturing Goodness: in the Church

1. Dietrich Bonhoeffer, *Letters and Papers from Prison*, The Enlarged Edition, SCM Press 1971, pp. 382f.

2. Frank Wright, *The Pastoral Nature of the Ministry*, SCM Press 1980, pp. 49–50.

8 · Nurturing Goodness: The Experience of C. S. Lewis

1. C. S. Lewis, *Christian Behaviour*, Geoffrey Bles 1943, p. 34.

2. Ibid., p. 31.

3. C. S. Lewis, *The Problem of Pain*, Geoffrey Bles 1940, p. 96.

4. Ibid., p. 141.

5. C. S. Lewis, *A Grief Observed*, Faber and Faber 1961, p. 10.

6. Ibid., p. 9.

7. C. S. Lewis, *Letters to Malcolm*, Geoffrey Bles 1963, p. 101.

9 · Nurturing Goodness: In the Young

1. Bruno Bettelheim, *The Uses of Enchantment*, Penguin 1978, pp. 9–10.

Epilogue

1. Arnold Schoenberg, *Style and Illusion*, Faber and Faber 1975, p. 447.

2. Robert Browning, Abt Vogler, 1X, in the *Poems of Robert Browning*, Oxford University Press 1925, p. 635.